MARK CARWARDINE'S
ULTIMATE WILDLIFE EXPERIENCES

⠿ WRITTEN AND PHOTOGRAPHED BY MARK CARWARDINE ⠿

www.UltimateWildlifeExperiences.com

FOREWORD
By Stephen Fry

There is a list of travelling-companion qualities that I would urge anyone to draw up before so much as thinking of sharing a short car ride with a stranger. Aside from issues of personal hygiene, the noises the other makes when sucking sweets, or how much and how loudly they impose their music collection on you, there is that unplannable deal-breaker: do each of you manage to adopt and adapt to the other's inevitable but unstoppable yearnings for silence or needs to chatter? Only nature/alchemy/fate can determine such unpredictable deal-breakers. And so far we are only talking about a short ride across a tiny island like Britain. These small things matter, but when you scale the journey up to a series of journeys, over months and years, to every corner of the earth by every means of transport from mule to ketch, from sea-plane to tuk-tuk, even the smallest and most innocent little tic or mannerism can be magnified beyond endurability.

I have put a girdle around the earth with Mark Carwardine many, many times now and can reveal that a finer travelling companion has yet to be born. There is simply nothing about him to dislike, expect possibly his ability to fall asleep in uncomfortable positions, which I envy enormously, and his unerring instinct for stepping out of a Land Rover and onto dry land, which is equally and exactly opposite to my instinct for stepping into a mountain of elephant dung or mosquito-infested puddle.

Mark Carwardine has been to more countries than anyone I have ever met. For many of the hundreds of thousand miles he has racked up, I have had the good fortune to be by his side. I cannot think of a single drawback in his character. He might, on occasion, be a little too willing to remember occasions when his light plane was tossed through malevolent thunderclouds like a paper dart just as we are about to take off into a storm cell the size of Scotland; there may be a trifle too much relish detectable in his voice as he describes the spiders bigger than laptops and the venomous puppy-sized centipedes that you will find on your face when you awaken in your tent, deep in the jungle that he is

so cheerfully guiding you towards. But when a man has been through much himself, undergone such deprivation, danger and disease and still lost not one scintilla of the original zeal, passion, commitment and wonderment that first plunged him into the world of wildlife and conservation, you can forgive him just about anything.

Mark doesn't travel light. This is not because he is inexperienced, unsure of local conditions, finicky about his appearance, an exotic camping equipment obsessive or fanatical about shoes for all seasons. No, he travels heavy because over the last 30 years he has become one of the world's leading wildlife photographers, and no matter how much technology might miniaturise this little thing or that, there is still no way to capture the astonished stare of an aye-aye or the backlit miracle of a humpback whale hurling its colossal weight up through the surface in one of nature's most astonishing and thrilling spectacles – the breach – without a collection of lenses and filters that most people would be unable to lift, let alone tote through jungles, deserts and swamps. I have some magnificent pictures of a blue whale fluking and a mountain gorilla cradling its baby. As snapshots, they remind me of intensely wonderful

moments. Mark's pictures are a whole other order of achievement. And they all spring from his greatest qualities. Knowledge. Patience. Persistence. Good humour. Courage. Indomitability.

These qualities take him on anti-poaching patrols where, cliché or not, death lurks around every corner. Friends and colleagues of his have been massacred in their tents by gangs of ruthless, heavily-armed poachers who will as happily machine-gun a band of conservationists as a herd of elephants or a family of tigers. This has never so much as given him pause, and his work goes on.

There's romance, beauty, variety, glory and an inexhaustible display of the miraculous in what Mark sees almost every month of every year, often in countries that you and I couldn't place on a globe to within a thousand miles. But there is danger and almost inevitable disappointment waiting too, as mankind expands its horizons at the expense of the biodiversity, habitat richness and survival of so many of the zones of the planet that contain the greatest and least understood forms of life.

People like Mark don't give up. They don't march, moan or shake their fists, much as they may sometimes want to. Instead Mark keeps, as the man says in that Robert Redford film *Jeremiah Johnson*, "his nose to the wind and his eye to the skyline", combining his conservation and anti-poaching work with the series of cruises to whale-and-dolphin-rich waters he annually organizes, where his expertise on all things marine and mammal changes the lives of those who book ahead (as book ahead they must for such an oversubscribed adventure). To have Mark lean over the bow of a boat, point to a sperm whale or bottlenose dolphin and describe with the excitement of a child and the authority of an expert exactly what it is that you are watching is a privilege few will be lucky to experience.

It is our good fortune that he is as fine and as exciting a writer as he is a photographer and adventurer. He will never give up. By buying this book, you will find out a little more about our world and be inspired to see some of the places and the shatteringly beautiful creatures that this remarkable man is battling to register, record and preserve.

My god does he snore though.

Stephen Fry, London, September 2011

CONTENTS

42 Bumbling around Borneo, Malaysia

More beauty and wildlife than you can possibly imagine, crammed into the ultimate biodiversity hotspot in a tiny corner of south-east Asia.

50 Lunching with Sea Otters, California, USA

Pick up some good vibrations with a spot of wildlife watching, California-style: from a window-seat in a West Coast diner.

54 Tracking Jaguars, Brazil

Explore South America's best-kept secret – the giant wetlands of the Pantanal – in search of its most famous inhabitant... and many of its neighbours.

62 Checking out the Chathams, New Zealand

Far from the madding crowd, this remote archipelago offers the last chance to see a motley collection of critically endangered wildlife.

66 Cruising with Polar Bears, Svalbard

With more bears than humans, this northern Norwegian outpost is the best place to encounter these beautiful – and formidable – animals.

72 Hanging around with Bats, Zambia

Go batty and see one of the greatest wildlife spectacles on earth – a twice-daily blizzard of no fewer than eight million flying foxes.

76 Running from Komodo Dragons, Indonesia

Share a tiny island with a host of venomous snakes and giant menacing lizards that could kill you with a single infectious bite.

84 Being hugged by Manatees, Florida, USA

While manatees aren't necessarily the most beautiful animals in the world, they are certainly among the most curious – and friendly.

88 Soaring with Seabirds, Iceland

There's wildlife in truly astonishing numbers all over Iceland's stark lunar landscapes – and there's plenty of elbow room for a little peace and quiet, too.

94 Leaping with Lemurs, Madagascar

Virtually all the weird and wonderful wildlife that lives here doesn't exist anywhere else: meet tenrecs, fosas, jabadys and an awful lot of lemurs.

102 Hovering with Hummingbirds, Arizona, USA

Live life in the fast lane: join 15 species of hummingbirds in the Huachuca Mountains and marvel at these iridescent 'bees on speed'.

106 Counting Penguins and Seals, South Georgia

Harsh, rugged, brutal. This speck in the immensity of the Southern Ocean is home to no fewer than 50 million seabirds and five million seals.

114 Pointing at Pachyderms, India

A face-to-horn encounter with one of the many – and surprisingly approachable – rhinos of Assam's oldest national park.

118 Encountering Great Whites, Mexico

A jaw-dropping encounter with the quintessential shark – the star of *Jaws* that gave all sharks such a terribly bad name.

122 Following in Darwin's Footsteps, Ecuador

Probably the most famous wildlife-watching destination in the world, the Galápagos are full to the brim with tame and approachable wildlife.

*For **Adam** & **Vanessa**,*
with love

Wanderlust

Published by Wanderlust Travel Media
Leworth Place, Mellor Walk, Windsor, SL4 1EB, UK
Tel: +44 (0)1753 620426
Fax: +44 (0)1753 620474
Web: www.wanderlust.co.uk
Email: info@wanderlust.co.uk

Editor-in-Chief & Publisher: **Lyn Hughes**
Editor: **Dan Linstead**
Art Director: **Graham Berridge**
Production Editor: **Tom Hawker**
Associate Editor: **Sarah Baxter**
Operations Director: **Danny Callaghan**

INTRODUCTION
By Mark Carwardine

Watching you, watching me: A wolf in Mongolia (which made it into the top 161, but not into the book)

This is a book about my favourite places in the world to watch wildlife. It's a personal selection of the wildlife hotspots that have made the greatest impact on me over the years, the wildlife-rich corners of the world that I return to time and time again, and miss the most when I'm somewhere else.

Despite 30 years spent travelling the world in search of wildlife and wild places, I can't claim to have been everywhere. There are still vast swathes of the planet I have yet to visit and umpteen different animals I have yet to see. I really should go to Cape May, in New Jersey, for instance, to witness what is reputed to be the greatest bird migration on the planet. I've spent weeks searching for Siberian tigers in the heart of their range in the Russian Far East, but I still haven't had the good fortune to see one of these endangered big cats in the wild.

And I've wanted to dive with thresher sharks in the Philippines for as long as I can remember.

Yet when I started to write this book, my original list of favourite places included no fewer than 161 different hotspots. I wanted to wax lyrical and rave about them all, but it was far too many. The whole point was to pick the really, really good places, my personal best of the best.

To do that, I had to be much more selective. But how can you compare sitting quietly next to a bright red flower, mesmerised by charismatic hummingbirds in iridescent suits, with the adrenalin rush of a face-to-face underwater encounter with a great white shark? And how can you compare a fleeting glimpse of a critically endangered Sumatran rhino with the spectacle of millions of monarch butterflies at their winter roost? All these wildlife encounters are riveting, exhilarating, uplifting and humbling experiences in their different ways.

But I had to whittle the list down somehow and there is some logic to my reasoning. I've tried to pick a diverse range of animals, a broad geographical spread and a wide variety of activities: from watching sea otters right outside the window of a restaurant in California to searching for Indian rhinos in a remote corner of India. By including polar bear watching in Svalbard, I've resisted the temptation to include, as well, polar bear watching on wonderful Baffin Island; I have begrudgingly left out the Great Barrier Reef, in favour of Borneo's magical Sipadan Island; and I've rejected thousands of seabirds wheeling and turning above their breeding cliffs on St. Kilda because the seabirds wheeling and turning above their breeding cliffs in Iceland just pipped them to the post.

I've resisted the overwhelming temptation to include more than one of my favourite whale-watching destinations, too, because they will be the subject of another book.

This Image: A dwarf minke whale off the Great Barrier Reef, Australia: the subject of another book

Right: A Sumatran rhino in Indonesia: almost impossible to see; an Amazon river dolphin, Brazil: too delicate for an onslaught of tourists

"I've tried to pick places that anyone can visit without having to sleep rough or stand for weeks waist-deep in mosquito-infested swamps"

So I'll be able to wax lyrical about close encounters with bubble-netting humpback whales in Southeast Alaska, watching southern right whales from a hotel bed in South Africa, and performing underwater ballets with Atlantic spotted dolphins in The Bahamas another time. Likewise, I'll be able to rave about some of my favourite African safaris – from Queen Elizabeth National Park, in Uganda, to the Okavango Delta, in Botswana – because they will make up a third book.

Throughout, I've tried to pick places that anyone can visit without having to organise special permits, charter planes, sleep rough or stand for weeks waist-deep in mosquito-infested swamps. I've also picked places where the chances of success are relatively high. For this reason, I haven't included tracking snow leopards in Mongolia (even though Mongolia is one of my favourite

countries), for instance, or searching for giant pandas in the bamboo forests of south-western China (I did once see a wild panda in the famed reserve at Wolong, but the odds are heavily stacked against it happening again).

There are never any guarantees in wildlife-watching, of course, and the anticipation – the not knowing – is all part of the fun. But in these days of global warming, with wildlife seasons and weather conditions frustratingly fickle, it's harder than ever to predict what is going to turn up, and when. So I have picked places and wildlife where the odds are firmly stacked in your favour.

Finally, there is another reason for dropping some very special places. Ten years ago, I would have included the great wildebeest river crossing in the Masai Mara, Kenya, for instance, or tiger-watching in India's Ranthambhore National Park. But I'm sorry to say that much of the magic of these places has evaporated with the sheer number of tourists and the outrageous lack of proper controls. Sadly, there is no doubt that unregulated tourism can damage the wildlife and wild places it seeks to celebrate.

But that's not to say that all ecotourism is bad. If I believed that to be true, I wouldn't have written this book. Far from it, I believe that responsible ecotourism can be an invaluable conservation tool. Quite simply, it makes wildlife worth more alive than dead, by raising much-needed foreign exchange for cash-strapped governments, providing employment for local people (everything from anti-poaching patrols in Malawi to carving wooden Komodo dragons to sell to tourists in Indonesia) and, managed properly, raising funds for the upkeep of national parks and reserves.

A classic example is the mountain gorilla. Without tourist dollars pouring into Uganda, Rwanda and the Democratic Republic of Congo, there is little doubt that mountain gorillas would not be around today. Tourists make gorilla conservation sustainable in the long-term.

But it's not just about making wildlife pay its way. Responsible ecotourism also helps to rekindle a concern for wildlife and a sense of wonderment that so many people seem to have lost. The more people who know about the special places in this book, and feel inspired to care about them, the better.

So here is the final selection. One thing I can guarantee is that none of them will disappoint. I've never known anyone return from an expedition cruise to South Georgia and say "It was OK", or from a week in the Pantanal and say "We didn't see very much". Hopefully, if you've been there already, they will bring back many happy memories, and, if you haven't, they will inspire you to go.

But these are also places to dream about. Nothing beats searching for whales with the wind in your hair, tracking lions with African dust clinging to your shoes, or standing next to penguins with your fingers numb with the cold, but sometimes just knowing that ring-tailed lemurs, spirit bears, manatees, great white sharks and all the other awe-inspiring, captivating, remarkable animals in this book are out there... is nearly enough.

Mark Carwardine, Bristol, 2011

The EXPERIENCES

SEEING GHOSTS

Canada: The Great Bear Rainforest

Imagine a black bear in a white coat silently emerging, ghost-like, from one of the most lush, rich and enchanting forests you will ever see

A bit of all white: A sighting of the spirit – or Kermode – bear on Princess Royal Island, the Great Bear Rainforest, British Columbia

The experience

What? Looking for spirit bears and other North American wildlife in an extremely remote and breathtaking wilderness twice the size of the Serengeti

Where? Princess Royal Island, on the west coast of British Columbia

How? Exploring aboard a small yacht or staying in a lodge

The Great Bear Rainforest is a breathtaking wilderness of ancient trees, fern-clad canyons, glacial waterfalls, rivers, streams and creeks, unnamed islands and islets, rocky headlands, coves, inlets and bays that stretches seamlessly from the northern end of Vancouver Island all the way to southeast Alaska. Covering an area more than twice the size of Belgium (25,000 square miles) and stretching for more than 250 miles down Canada's west coast, it is the largest remaining tract of intact temperate rainforest left in the world.

It is sometimes called Canada's Amazon and is an awe-inspiring place to explore. One day you might be hiking through the shadowy forest, darkened by the sun-blocking canopy of some of the oldest and largest trees on earth: Sitka spruce, red cedar and western hemlock (some nearly

My best day

I remember spending several hours on a wooden observation platform on Gribbell Island, overlooking the Ryordan River. I'd been sitting quietly, listening to the gentle patter of rain on the makeshift tarpaulin roof, while swatting huge, buzzing clouds of 'no-see-ums' – miniscule insects with surprisingly painful bites. Every so often an American marten would run across the track or a Sitka deer would peer out of the forest. Occasionally, a black bear wandered down to fish. Then an apparition appeared on the riverbank, looking straight at me. It was my first ever spirit bear and it really did feel as if I had seen a ghost.

1,000 years old and 300 feet tall). The next day you could be walking along the lower, slower reaches of a river tracking wolves and bears (wolves eat just the head of a salmon and leave the rest, while bears eat the rest and leave the head). You could be crawling around on your hands and knees, studying banana slugs or marvelling at the multi-coloured starfish in coastal rock pools. Or you could be in a small boat or kayak, cruising past a boisterous summer rookery of hundreds of Steller sea lions, watching humpback whales fishing with nets made of bubbles, or following a pod of orcas hunting along the coast. Then, at night, reminiscing about the sights of the day, you could be sitting on the deck of your yacht, or the veranda of your lodge, listening to the silence punctuated only by howling wolves and wailing loons. It is out of this world.

The Great Bear Rainforest is packed full of wildlife and has a biological productivity that rivals many tropical rainforests. It has

one of the highest concentrations of bears in North America (including nearly half of Canada's grizzlies and some of the largest bears on the continent) and a significant population of grey wolves. There are 68 mammal species altogether, from river otters and American martens to cougars and mountain goats. It is also home to no fewer than 230 species of birds – bald eagles, pileated woodpeckers, brown creepers, tufted puffins, marbled murrelets and Cassin's auklets among them – including five million seabirds of 15 species that breed in the coastal waters in summer. It also provides a rest stop and refuelling station for millions of migratory birds travelling along the Pacific Flyway every spring and autumn.

Pacific salmon are the lifeblood of the region. There are five species here (chinook, coho, pink, chum and sockeye) and they are largely responsible for the forest's health and productivity. The salmon hatch in the gravel beds of

innumerable creeks, streams and rivers, swim out to sea and then return in their hundreds of thousands, two-to-seven years later, to spawn and die in the waters where they were born. Watching the salmon runs is a true wildlife spectacle in itself and this annual surge of food enables all those bears to fatten up and survive their winter hibernation.

The white black bear

The jewel in the Great Bear Rainforest's crown is a very special animal that is found nowhere else on the planet. The spirit bear is elusive and rarely seen – except for a few weeks every year in one tiny corner of the forest. Also known as the ghost bear, or Kermode bear (named after Francis Kermode, former director of the Royal British Columbia Museum), it is one of the most awe-inspiring and enigmatic animals on the planet.

It may be predominantly white or creamy white (it was once described as

A walk in the park: Clambering over rocks on Gribbell Island, a spirit bear makes a very rare appearance out in the open

Left: A spirit bear successfully catches a salmon in the Ryordan River; a black bear does a spot of fishing in the waters of Princess Royal Island; a bald eagle flies in front of a storm at Prince Rupert; an aerial view of the Great Bear Rainforest reveals how dense it is

SPECIES CHECKLIST

- Spirit bear
- Black bear
- Grizzly bear
- Grey wolf
- Wolverine
- American marten
- Mink
- Sitka deer
- Northern river otter
- Steller sea lion
- Harbour seal
- Fin whale
- Humpback whale
- Orca
- Pacific white-sided dolphin
- Dall's porpoise
- Bald eagle
- Great northern diver
- Pigeon guillemot
- Rhinoceros auklet

… and many more

"Legend has it that good fortune rewards anyone lucky enough to encounter a spirit bear – it certainly feels that way"

'more like a vanilla-coloured carpet in need of a steam-clean') but it is neither polar bear nor albino. It has normal pigmentation in its eyes, nose and skin. In fact, it's a walking contradiction – a white black bear – an extremely rare colour variant of the American black bear. The whiteness comes from a recessive gene and so, to be born white, the bear must inherit the gene from both parents. This means that, in a strange twist of nature, a spirit bear's parents can both be black.

Native legend, however, has a more intriguing explanation. It tells the story of the Raven, the Creator, who came from heaven during the last Ice Age to make the world green. On a visit to Princess Royal Island, the Raven made every tenth bear white as a reminder of the snow and ice, and designated this little corner of Canada's 'forgotten coast' as the home of the spirit bear forever. Spirit bears play

Below: Viewing platforms in the rainforest make sightings easier

a supremely important role in Gitga'at mythology (the Gitga'at First Nation people live in the village of Hartley Bay, in the heart of spirit bear country) and legend has it that good fortune rewards anyone lucky enough to encounter them. It certainly feels that way.

No one can agree on exactly how many spirit bears are lurking in the Great Bear Rainforest. Some say as few as 100, others as many at 1,000. But the figure is probably around 400 or fewer.

The heart of their range is Princess Royal Island and neighbouring Gribbell Island. There are believed to be about 400 black bears on Princess Royal altogether – of which 40 are white. On Gribbell, one in three is white. Why they aren't more widespread had puzzled scientists, but recent research may have come up with an answer. It seems that white bears are less visible to fish than their black counterparts, making them 30% more efficient at capturing salmon. But there is a price to pay – whiteness also makes them more vulnerable to grizzlies and wolves, which frequently kill black bears.

So how do you see a spirit bear? First, you have to go to the Princess-Gribbell area. Second, you have to go in September. Spirit bears spend the winter fast asleep, and most of their waking life hiding in the dark, tangled recesses of the forest. Even when their cousins, the black bears, are out in the open feeding on sedge grass during May and June, the region's most famous

and enigmatic inhabitants are seldom seen. Spirit bears are occasionally seen at other times of the year, but usually by people who live and work in the forest all their lives. In reality, the chances of seeing a spirit bear are extremely slim, unless you go during the few weeks each autumn when they leave the forest and venture out into the open to gorge on the spawning salmon. Then your chances are good.

Concern for the future

While over half the world's temperate rainforests have already been destroyed,

Catching some rays: A congregation of Steller sea lions makes the most of the sunshine in the heart of the Great Bear Rainforest

Need to know

WHEN TO GO

The best time for wildlife in the Great Bear Rainforest – and really the only time to see spirit bears – is **September**. For a few weeks every autumn, hundreds of creeks, streams and rivers teem with spawning and dying salmon and it is this surge of food that attracts the bears, as well as wolves, river otters, bald eagles and a host of other wildlife, out of the forest. **Orcas** are feeding on salmon in the inlets and channels around Princess Royal Island mainly in May, June and early July; **humpback whales** feed in the area all summer but especially in September.

HOW TO DO IT

Princess Royal Island is the epicentre of spirit bear distribution, but the white bears are also found on Gribbell, Pooley, Roderick and adjacent islands, and there are even a few on the nearby mainland. There are observation platforms on the Ryordan River (Gribbell).

The **Great Bear Rainforest** is true wilderness, with no trains and no real roads. Getting around involves planes – usually floatplanes – or boats. Thus this can be an expensive area to visit and, unless you have your own boat, it's difficult to explore independently.

There are three choices. First is a wonderful **eco-sensitive wilderness lodge** called King Pacific Lodge, in Barnard Harbor on the north-west coast of Princess Royal Island. Resembling an outsize ski chalet, this floating lodge is about as luxurious as it gets. But to all intents and purposes it is in the middle of nowhere – and, consequently, has everything from river otters and bald eagles to spirit bears and humpback whales right on the doorstep. Fly from Vancouver north to the little settlement of Bella Bella, then transfer to a small floatplane to be delivered right to the door of the lodge.

Second is **Spirit Bear Lodge** on the north-west coast of Swindle Island; again, access is via Bella Bella (with an overnight in Shearwater).

Alternatively, at Bella Bella you can join a **live-aboard yacht**, with daily excursions by kayak, in inflatable Zodiacs and on foot.

the wonderful Great Bear Rainforest has survived into the 21st century relatively intact. But in recent years British Columbia's voracious timber industry has turned its attentions to the region and vast holes have started to appear in the once-pristine wilderness.

Canada's logging industry already has an appalling track record and, left to its own devices, would liquidate an entire 10,000-year-old virgin forest in less than a human lifetime. In fact, the Great Bear Rainforest is known in government and logging circles as 'the Mid and North Coast Timber Supply Area'. The region is also under threat from the Northern Gateway Pipeline Project that, if approved, would bring crude oil tanker traffic passing regularly through the channels of the forest.

Conservation groups and First Nation communities (who have been stewards of the 'forgotten coast' for thousands of years) are fighting all these threats. Perhaps it's unrealistic to wish that every last tree can be saved, but I believe that the Great Bear Rainforest is such a special place it should really be sacrosanct.

Boof! Humpbacks put on spectacular acrobatic displays while greys (*inset*) like to be tickled

Meeting friendly
GIANTS

Mexico: Baja California

Tickle a grey whale, listen to a humpback's song and marvel at the biggest creature on the planet: Baja California is simply sensational for cetaceans

The experience

What: The world's best place for whale watching: a kaleidoscope of greys and blues

Where: The spindly peninsula that divides mainland Mexico from the Pacific Ocean

How: Fly to San Diego, California, and join a two-week live-aboard boat, or head for San Ignacio, Mexico, and take day trips

Look at a map of North America and, down in the bottom left-hand corner, you will see a long stretch of land that looks rather like a giant chilli. This is Baja California – my favourite place for whale watching.

Over the years, I've been to most of the top whale-watching destinations around the world – and there are some wonderful spots among them – but Baja is the place I return to time and time again. I've been visiting this wild corner of Mexico one, two or three times a year since the late 1980s and it's always utterly breathtaking.

With a little luck, in a two-week trip, you can tickle implausibly friendly grey whales under the chin, listen to humpback whales singing their haunting, unearthly songs, enjoy unforgettably close encounters with gargantuan blue whales, travel with thousands of boisterous common dolphins,

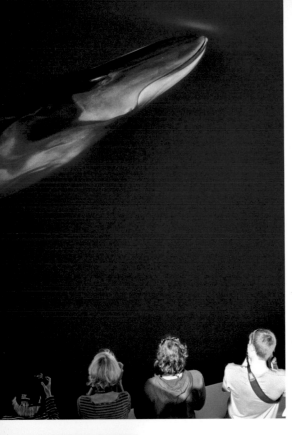

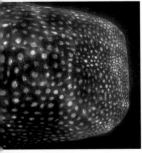

Top left: Fin whales are the second-biggest creatures on the planet

Top right: The Sea of Cortez is a whale soup, home to many species including short-finned pilot whales

Above: Whale sharks – about as dangerous as a big spotty tadpole

and see a host of other species from sei whales and sperm whales to Dall's porpoises and Peruvian beaked whales. Along the way, you can snorkel with playful California sea lions, rare Guadalupe fur seals and even whale sharks; go beachcombing on remote subtropical islands; explore spectacular cactus forests; and marvel at bioluminescent seas.

One of the longest peninsulas in the world, stretching 800 miles south from the Californian border, Baja is unusual because it is both a breeding ground and a feeding ground for great whales. This means that you can see a greater variety of species in a couple of weeks here than almost anywhere else on the planet.

The setting is truly wonderful, too, with over 1,800 miles of untamed shoreline, no fewer than seven impressive mountain ranges, and vast, almost uninhabitable deserts. But best of all, Baja is gloriously peaceful and serene. There are very few whale-watching boats in the region and so,

most of the time, you have the whales and dolphins all to yourself. As John Steinbeck writes in his classic *The Log from the Sea of Cortez*: 'Whatever it is that makes one aware that men are about is not there. Thus, in spite of the noises of waves and fishes, one has a feeling of... quietness.'

San Ignacio Lagoon

The Pacific side of this 'Mexican Galápagos' is best known as the winter home of practically the entire world population of grey whales. Safely sheltered from the pounding surf of the open ocean, thousands of them gather to socialise, mate and calve in a string of magical, mangrove-lined lagoons beside the desert.

Once on the verge of extinction, grey whales have bounced back thanks to intensive conservation efforts. Now as many as 21,000 of these inveterate travellers migrate backwards and forwards along the entire length of the western North American coastline, between their

feeding grounds in the Arctic and their breeding grounds in Baja. The round-trip distance can be as much as 12,500 miles, making their journey one of the longest migrations of any mammal.

They gather in four main breeding lagoons in Baja: Guerrero Negro, Ojo de Liebre (Scammon's Lagoon), Magdalena Bay and San Ignacio. My favourite is San Ignacio, which is home to the world-famous 'friendlies'.

Just a few days in San Ignacio can be thrilling, uplifting and all-round life-changing. The grey whales here literally nudge the sides of the small whale-watching boats (pangas) and lie alongside waiting to be scratched and tickled. It's a breathless and, initially, rather nerve-wracking experience but it's arguably one of the greatest wildlife encounters on earth.

It's hard to believe that these very same grey whales once had a reputation for being ferocious. They were hunted ruthlessly in the late 19th and early 20th centuries, until

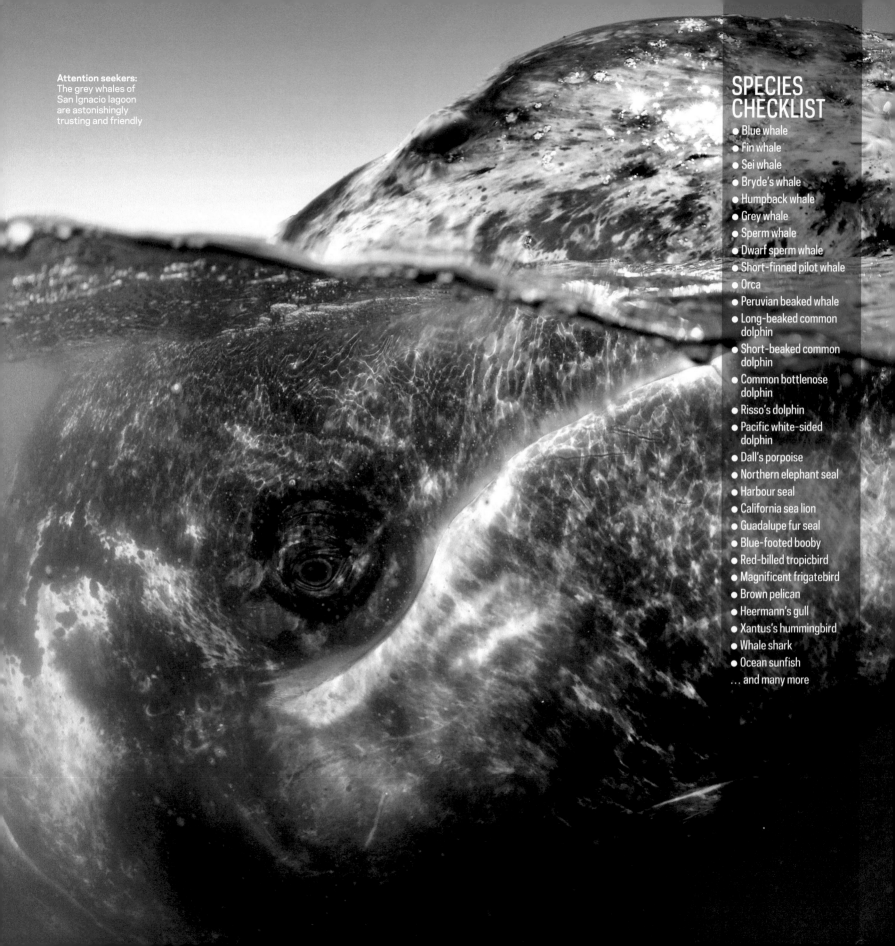

Attention seekers:
The grey whales of
San Ignacio lagoon
are astonishingly
trusting and friendly

SPECIES CHECKLIST

- Blue whale
- Fin whale
- Sei whale
- Bryde's whale
- Humpback whale
- Grey whale
- Sperm whale
- Dwarf sperm whale
- Short-finned pilot whale
- Orca
- Peruvian beaked whale
- Long-beaked common dolphin
- Short-beaked common dolphin
- Common bottlenose dolphin
- Risso's dolphin
- Pacific white-sided dolphin
- Dall's porpoise
- Northern elephant seal
- Harbour seal
- California sea lion
- Guadalupe fur seal
- Blue-footed booby
- Red-billed tropicbird
- Magnificent frigatebird
- Brown pelican
- Heermann's gull
- Xantus's hummingbird
- Whale shark
- Ocean sunfish

… and many more

"The air is filled with the humpback's baffling medley of moans and squeaks, which makes the hairs on the back of your neck stand on end"

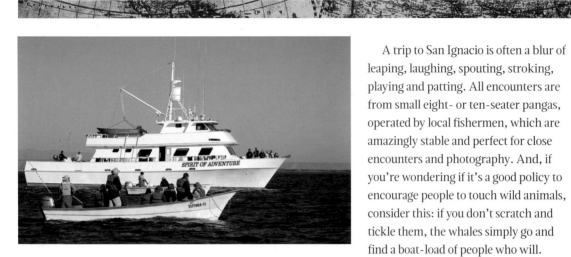

Underwater whirled: Los Islotes is the world's best spot to snorkel with California sea lions

Top right: Guadalupe fur seals squabbling at San Benitos

Bottom right: Bottlenose dolphins frequently play around the boat in the Sea of Cortez

Above: Small pangas (fishing boats) are the best way to get close whale encounters in San Ignacio lagoon

Below: Mobula rays launch themselves over 3 feet out of the sea

there were almost none left. Yankee whalers entered the Baja lagoons in small wooden rowing boats (roughly the same size as today's whale-watching pangas) and harpooned them. But the whales fought back – chasing the whaling boats, lifting them out of the water like big rubber ducks, ramming them with their heads and dashing them to pieces with their tails. They would 'fight like devils', so the Yankee whalers dubbed them 'devilfish'.

Nowadays, the survivors positively welcome whale-watching tourists into their breeding lagoons. Somehow, they seem to understand that we come in peace and, far from smashing our small boats to smithereens, welcome us with open flippers. They are as trusting and playful as kittens – albeit kittens up to 50-foot long. They seem to have forgiven us for all those years of greed, recklessness and cruelty. They trust us, when we don't really deserve to be trusted. It's a humbling experience.

A trip to San Ignacio is often a blur of leaping, laughing, spouting, stroking, playing and patting. All encounters are from small eight- or ten-seater pangas, operated by local fishermen, which are amazingly stable and perfect for close encounters and photography. And, if you're wondering if it's a good policy to encourage people to touch wild animals, consider this: if you don't scratch and tickle them, the whales simply go and find a boat-load of people who will.

There are bottlenose dolphins in San Ignacio, too. I feel sorry for them: elsewhere in the world, they get heaps of attention but, in San Ignacio, they're competing with the friendliest whales in the world.

Pacific Coast

The easiest way to explore Baja is by boat, and the best trips leave from San Diego, southern California, cruising all the way down the Pacific coast before turning into the Sea of Cortez. San Ignacio is obviously a highlight, but there's even more to this wild and rugged side of the peninsula.

Whale watching can be outstandingly good here; it is possible to see a wide variety of species. Bryde's, sei, fin, humpback and blue whales are all commonly seen – the area off Magdalena Bay is a particularly important feeding ground for blues – as well as short-beaked common, long-beaked common, bottlenose, Pacific white-sided and Risso's dolphins, and Dall's porpoises. But almost anything can turn up.

There are also some interesting stop-offs en route. The best is an archipelago called San Benitos – three islands imaginatively called West, Central and East – which is a superb spot for seals and sea lions. The largest island, West, is probably the most productive: you can get up close to northern elephant seals, whose rookeries are everywhere.

It is also one of the few places in the world to see Guadalupe fur seals. Once so rare that they were actually declared extinct, Guadalupe fur seals have been brought back from the brink and are slowly expanding their range. Until recently they bred only on Guadalupe, a tiny island 150

miles away in the Pacific (see 'Encountering Great Whites', on page 118), but they first appeared in San Benitos in 1997 and quickly gained a foothold. Now there are believed to be a few thousand of them in the archipelago and they can easily be seen on rocks all around the coast.

Gorda Banks

Just off the southern tip of Baja California is another magical whale hotspot: a breeding ground for humpbacks. There are two underwater seamounts here – Inner and Outer Gorda Banks – which are where the whales like to gather. The best area tends to be off the sandy beach of Los Frailes.

If you wanted to design the perfect whale for whale-watching, you couldn't do much better than a humpback. It's not too difficult to find, nice and easy to identify, shamelessly inquisitive and capable of performing some of the most spectacular acrobatic displays on earth.

One of the highlights of a visit here is the chance to listen to male humpback whales singing their plaintive songs. Drop an underwater microphone, or hydrophone, into the water and the air is filled with a baffling medley of moans, groans, snores, squeaks and whistles that makes the hairs on the back of your neck stand on end. With elements of jazz, bebop, blues, heavy

metal, classical and reggae all rolled into one, this mesmerising, unforgettable live concert is the longest and most complex song in the animal kingdom and sparks a rollercoaster of emotions.

Sea of Cortez

Rounding the Baja peninsula, turning north, you enter an even more extraordinary world. This is the Sea of Cortez, or Gulf of California, which lies between Baja and 'mainland' Mexico. It is a well-kept secret that tends to be overshadowed by San Ignacio, its more famous neighbour. But visiting the grey whale lagoons without venturing into the

"Swimming with a whale shark is not quite as safe as watching breakfast television – but it comes pretty close"

Sea of Cortez is like buying a book and then reading only the first chapter.

Dotted with islands that harbour huge numbers of magnificent frigatebirds, red-billed tropicbirds, blue-footed boobies and many other seabirds, the Sea of Cortez is also home to weird and wonderful elephant trees, the world's tallest cactuses, endemic Xantus's hummingbirds, mobula rays that leap out of the water like flying pancakes, ocean sunfish, several different species of sea turtles, and so much more. There is even a little islet, called Los Islotes, that is probably the best place in the world to snorkel with friendly, inquisitive and playful California sea lions.

But it's the whales that draw people back time and again: Bryde's whales (this is one of the best places in the world to find

Below: Baja is one of the only places where sightings of blue whales are virtually guaranteed

them), fin whales, sperm whales, short-finned pilot whales, dwarf sperm whales and all sorts of other species.

Of course, there's also the largest animal on the planet. The Sea of Cortez is one of the few places in the world where blue whales are virtually guaranteed. Hundreds of thousands of them were killed by whalers and, although they were given official protection in the mid-1960s, most populations have never recovered. But there is one group that seems to be thriving. Dividing its time between Baja California, central and southern California, and a place called the Costa Rica Dome (an upwelling of cold, nutrient-rich water off the coast of Central America), it accounts for as many as one in three of all the blue whales in the world. There are believed to be 2,000-3,000 in the region altogether.

It's impossible to prepare someone for their first encounter with a blue whale. It's stupendously, breathtakingly enormous: almost as long as a Boeing 737 and weighing as much as the entire human population of the Isles of Scilly (2,000 people). Seeing the largest and most impressive animal on earth is every naturalist's dream. A close encounter with just one blue whale makes any trip to Baja more than worthwhile.

Whale sharks in La Paz Bay

La Paz Bay is a colossal bite out of the south-eastern corner of the Baja peninsula and is among the best places in the world for close encounters with whale sharks. After years of being hunted intensively, the largest fish in the sea has all but disappeared from many of its former haunts in warm, temperate and tropical waters worldwide. But La Paz Bay is one of a handful of places where it is still found in reasonable numbers.

An intriguing assortment of juveniles and adults can be seen in the bay; it is not unknown to encounter as many as a dozen individuals in a single day. There is considerable confusion about their arrival and departure times, and no obvious pattern to their visits and movements

Close encounters:
Taking a live-aboard
boat trip is the best way
to see the whales,
including inquisitive
humpbacks

Need to know

WHEN TO GO

The main whale-watching season is from **early February to the end of April** (although fin whales, sperm whales, Bryde's whales and many dolphins are resident in the Sea of Cortez). There is no 'best' month since each has its own features and qualities. There tend to be many more **grey whales** in San Ignacio earlier in the season, while there is usually more friendly behaviour later in the season. **Whale shark** numbers peak September to mid-December; water visibility is worst January and February.

HOW TO DO IT

By far the best way to explore Baja – and see most of its whales and other wildlife - is to join a 12-day **marine safari**, sharing a self-contained boat with a small group of like-minded people. Most trips depart **San Diego, California**, travel down the entire Pacific coast of Baja, spend nearly a week in the Sea of Cortez, and then disembark in Cabo San Lucas, on the southern tip of the peninsula. There are also live-aboard trips departing **La Paz**, although these explore only the Sea of Cortez.

Alternatively, it's possible to **drive or fly** (from San Diego or Ensenada) to San Ignacio Lagoon and stay in one of several **camps on shore**. Local fishermen take you out in their

pangas to watch the whales every day, and you can lie in bed listening to the evocative sound of their blows at night. Half-day whale-watching tours are available in the other breeding lagoons, too.

There are also half-day and **full-day whale-watching trips** from Cabo San Lucas and Loreto, to look for humpback whales and blue whales respectively, while the delightful town of La Paz is a good base for **snorkelling** with California sea lions and whale sharks in La Paz Bay.

within the bay. The best time is generally considered to be September to mid-December, although tours run whenever the sharks are around and, indeed, they may be present in varying numbers year-round (outside the peak period, I have had excellent encounters in March, April, June and July). Where they go between visits to La Paz is one of the world's great wildlife mysteries.

The best way to find them is with the help of a spotter plane. They are much easier to locate from the air – from 600ft they look like giant, spotty tadpoles – and the pilot can then direct your boat to exactly the right place. You can observe them

without getting your feet wet but it's best to get in the water. Ask lots of questions before you book a snorkelling trip, and be careful to choose an operator that adheres to voluntary guidelines for hands-off underwater encounters, causing as little disturbance as possible to the sharks; beware those that do not.

Snorkelling with a whale shark is not quite as safe as watching breakfast television – simply because, in theory, any animal the length and weight of a bus is powerful enough to knock a mere, measly human clean out of the water. But it comes pretty close. Quite simply, it is one of life's highlights.

Taking a peak: Some mountain gorillas in Bwindi Impenetrable National Park have been habituated to receive human visitors

Rubbing shoulders with
MOUNTAIN GORILLAS

Uganda: Bwindi Impenetrable National Park

Gorilla-watching isn't always easy, but as Stephen Fry put it: "It's worth every sobbing, gasping, aching step of horror, sweat and humiliation. Wonderful."

The experience

What? Dropping in to see the relatives

Where? The south-western corner of Uganda, on the border with the Democratic Republic of Congo

How? Trek into the jungle with a team of trackers, guides, armed guards and porters

It's only an hour – and there is an awful lot of travelling and trekking to be done beforehand. But it is likely to be one of the most emotional, humbling and exhilarating hours of your life. Rubbing shoulders with wild mountain gorillas is a true privilege and, if everyone could do it just once, the world would be a better place.

The business of gorilla tourism is a vexed one. I know people who have always wanted to see gorillas, but have worried that tourism might be causing disturbance or exposing the animals to human disease. But in truth the gorillas probably wouldn't be here at all without tourism. It is the one thing that can guarantee their survival, by making them worth more alive than dead – to governments and local people alike.

There are currently about 800 mountain gorillas left in Africa: 480 in the Virunga

Volcanoes, which straddle Uganda, Rwanda and the Democratic Republic of Congo (DRC), and some 310-340 in Bwindi Impenetrable Forest, Uganda.

The Virunga Volcanoes is the place most people imagine when they think of mountain gorillas. Thirty-six family groups (and 14 solitary silverbacks) are distributed across three different protected areas: Volcanoes National Park, in Rwanda; Mgahinga Gorilla National Park, in Uganda; and Virunga National Park, in the DRC. But the gorilla-watching opportunities are actually quite limited. It's a little hit-and-miss in the DRC because, unhappily, the animals have been caught in a vortex of human conflict and misery and are forced to share their home with a motley collection of rebels and heavily-armed soldiers. Meanwhile, the only habituated group in Uganda's Mgahinga has a reputation for crossing the border into Rwanda and the DRC, so it is not a reliable spot for viewing either. That leaves Volcanoes National Park, in Rwanda, which has eight habituated gorilla groups

My best day

I remember searching for the Rushegura group, which had 14 family members. We were incredibly lucky and, just 35 minutes into the trek, our guides signalled for us to keep quiet. There, standing in plain view, was something so big that I hadn't even noticed it. It was a silverback. We followed the group down the hillside, to within 100 yards of my lodge. I could almost have watched them from my bed. But the best bit was that I saw them again later that afternoon, on the forest path immediately behind the garden. This time there were 15: in the few hours since my 'official' visit, one of the females had had a baby.

and is generally considered to be the hotspot for gorilla-watching.

But I really like lesser-known Bwindi Impenetrable Forest, a discrete area some 15-20 miles to the north. Bwindi is a tiny island of 128 square miles of equatorial primeval rainforest, surrounded by a sea of banana and tea plantations. A vast, misty, mountainous jungle, it is one of the most biologically diverse places in the world.

Although it can be difficult to spot much wildlife through the mass of huge trees festooned with vines and creepers, this forest is home to no fewer than 120 species of mammal, 360 birds, 310 butterflies and 1,000 different flowering plants. As you walk the trails, you are greeted at every turn by a cacophony of animal sounds.

But mountain gorillas are obviously the star attraction. The Uganda Wildlife Authority has habituated seven gorilla families to receive human visitors. These consist of as few as seven animals to as many as 36, led by a mature male or 'silverback' along with his harem of several females, various immature 'blackback' males, and youngsters.

The first to be habituated was the Mubare group, which was formally

SPECIES CHECKLIST

- Mountain gorilla
- Chimpanzee
- Red-tailed monkey
- L'Hoest's monkey
- Black-and-white colobus monkey
- Red colobus monkey
- Blue monkey
- Olive baboon
- Bushpig
- Forest duiker
- Grey-cheeked mangabey
- Black bee-eater
- Cinnamon-chested bee-eater
- Black-and-white casqued hornbill
- White-thighed hornbill
- Black-billed turaco
- Great blue turaco
- African green broadbill
- Montane oriole
- Black-faced rufous warbler
- Blue-headed coucal
- African paradise flycatcher
- Blue mother-of-pearl butterfly
- Cream-banded swallowtail
- East African giant swallowtail
… and many more

introduced to people for the first time in 1991; it's a popular family with tourists, because it spends much of its time fairly close to the park headquarters. The others are the Habinyanja, Nkuringo, Nshongi, Bitukura, Kyaguriro and Rushegura groups (unfortunately, the Rushegura group sometimes wanders out of Uganda and into the DRC, which causes havoc with treks booked months in advance).

Every morning, the latest influx of tourists gathers on the lawns near the forest entrance for a detailed briefing, before setting off chaperoned by trackers, guides, armed guards and porters.

"The Impenetrable Forest is aptly named – it's a riot of green where things grow on top of other things that grow on top of more things"

Get close up to our distant relatives: There are only 800 mountain gorillas left in Africa and access to them is tightly controlled

Left: A young gorilla keeps a mindful watch; the mysterious Bwindi Impenetrable rainforest; the super-human porters await their next task

Need to know

WHEN TO GO

Gorilla treks operate **year-round**. Jungle trails are easier to hike during the drier seasons (though heavy downpours are possible at any time of year); however, gorillas love to sunbathe after showers, so they often spend more time in the open during the **wet season**.

January to February and June to August are the driest months. **Daytime temperatures** average a pleasant 25-27°C (80-85°F), but it can get very cold at night. Some roads are **impassable** from March to May. June and July are best for butterflies, and many orchids flower in September and October.

HOW TO DO IT

Fly to Entebbe, then drive to Bwindi (320 miles of mostly tarmac but some very rough roads – **it takes a long day** and is easiest in a 4WD). Alternatively, charter a small plane from Kaijansi or Entebbe to Kayonza airstrip (about 1.5 hours). There are several lodges, tented camps, community rooms and campgrounds in Buhoma, near the park headquarters. Take gardening gloves for grasping nettles and thorny branches.

Gorilla-watching permits currently cost US$500 (US$350 in low season) for each trek and need to be booked well in advance. Each gorilla family can be visited only once a day, for a **no-quibble one hour, by a party of maximum eight people**.

There are no guarantees of an encounter, although the success rate is close to 100%. The biggest risk is that the gorillas will be in the treetops (where, in Bwindi, they spend about one-tenth of their time). You must be healthy – anyone with a cold, for instance, is banned from a close encounter with a gorilla – and relatively fit. The **high-altitude hikes can be tough**, with slopes, vines and mud. But just remember that the allotted hour will be one of the best of your life.

While you are in this corner of Uganda, don't miss **Queen Elizabeth NP**. Home to the world's largest concentration of hippos, thousands of Uganda kob, tree-climbing lions and some 550 bird species, this is one of the loveliest parks in Africa.

The super-human porters will carry anything – no amount of camera equipment is too much. The trek can take anything from less than an hour, if you're lucky, to as long as 11 hours, if you're not. It all depends on where your allotted gorilla family happens to be at the time.

Within minutes of entering the forest you are sweating and panting, crawling and clambering your way along slippery paths and precipitous mountain tracks. The dark, wet Impenetrable Forest is aptly-named – it's a riot of green where things grow on top of other things that grow on top of more things in layers of ferns, mosses, creepers and lichens. In places, the forest is so thick you have to hike on solid mats of vegetation that tremble and flex with every step, threatening to break through and dump you into the unseen depths below.

It's all very exciting. And the moment you come face-to-face with your first gorilla, the mud, the sweat and the tears are a distant memory. Standing in the heart of a seemingly limitless jungle, with a family of the largest primates in the world, is one of life's greatest pleasures. Your allotted hour – the maximum time allowed – goes so quickly it feels as if it has only just begun. But life will never be quite the same again.

Lolling on ice: Crabeater seals chill out on floes all over the Antarctic Peninsula

Right: You can see where the chinstrap penguin got its name

Freezing with the
PENGUINS

Antarctic Peninsula & the South Shetland Islands

The scale and magnificence of Antarctica has a powerful magnetism: I have been visiting for 20 years – and see no end in sight

The experience

What? A wildlife-packed adventure in the last great wilderness on earth

Where? The most accessible parts of Antarctica: the Antarctic Peninsula and the South Shetland Islands

How? A comfortable expedition aboard a ship with a specially strengthened hull

There is something very special, almost spiritual, about Antarctica. When asked why he returned there again and again to bitter cold and uncertain survival, Frank Wild (second-in-command of Ernest Shackleton's famed *Endurance* expedition of 1914-16), said he couldn't escape the 'little voices'. It's hard to explain to anyone who hasn't already been there, but the same little voices call many people back to the White Continent time and time again.

Nothing prepares you for the sheer beauty of the place: it bombards you with sensory overload at every turn. Imagine cruising in an inflatable Zodiac among otherworldly ice formations; mingling with fur seals as they assert their dominance on wild and desolate beaches; sitting alongside rookeries of noisy penguins; watching families of orcas patrolling the rugged

Above: Close encounters with crabeater seals are virtually guaranteed

Below: The chinstrap is probably the commonest penguin in the Antarctic, with about eight million pairs around the Antarctic Peninsula

coast; or simply taking time to enjoy the breathtaking scenery of ice-choked waterways, glaciers, blue and white icebergs, and snow-covered mountains. Not only is it home to the greatest concentration of wildlife in the world, Antarctica also provides a spectacular icy setting that lends the animals an incredible air of magnificence and majesty.

It's exceptional for other reasons, too. No country owns any part of the continent. The UK, Norway, France, Argentina, Chile, New Zealand and Australia all have territorial claims, which have been 'frozen' by the Antarctic Treaty, but the entire continent belongs to no one.

A number of babies have been born there – the first was Emilio Marcos de Palma, born at the Argentinian base, Esperanza, on 7 January 1978. It is home to about 1,100 scientists and support personnel in winter; up to 5,000 in summer. But there is no native population and no one lives there permanently.

Even better, despite all the remoteness and wildness, you can get to the Antarctic Peninsula region, explore a sizeable chunk of it, and get home again in little more than two weeks. The same journey a century ago would have demanded no less than two or three years – and you may not have come back alive.

Drake Passage

The journey begins and ends in the southernmost city in the world – Ushuaia, in Tierra del Fuego, Argentina – which nestles between the spectacular snow-capped mountains of the Andes and the famous Beagle Channel. It's worth arriving a day or two early to explore this interesting frontier town and to see South American fur seals, South American sea lions, Magellanic penguins, dolphin gulls, chimango caracaras, and some of the other local wildlife that you won't see further south.

Your ship will pass Cape Horn in the dark and head south, spending the whole of the next day and most of the day after that crossing the infamous Drake Passage. No amount of wishful thinking will make it otherwise. This 500 miles of open ocean between the southernmost tip of South America and the South Shetland Islands is notorious as one of the roughest bodies of water in the world. But I've had many glorious crossings with barely a swell, and

it can be one of the highlights of the trip. Whether you experience the calm 'Drake Lake' or the rough 'Drake Shake', the trick is to make the most of it. Be mesmerised by the immensity of the Southern Ocean, imagine following in the wake of early explorers, enjoy all the albatrosses, petrels and other seabirds accompanying your ship, and watch for the blows of great whales.

Over the years, I have seen a fantastic variety of cetaceans on Drake crossings: Hourglass, Peale's and southern right whale dolphins; orcas and long-finned pilot whales; sperm whales; humpback, fin and sei whales; Antarctic and dwarf minke whales; southern right whales; and even southern bottlenose whales. But a lot depends on weather and sea conditions – and search effort. Just remember: you won't see anything if you're not out there looking. If you do make the effort, you'll soon discover that two days on the Drake just isn't long enough.

South Shetland Islands

The first stop is usually an archipelago of 11 main islands and many smaller ones, stretching some 335 miles roughly parallel to the northern end of the Antarctic Peninsula. This is the warmest, wettest and most colourful part of the continent. It is where you will see your first enormous penguin rookeries, find out what it is like to land on beaches ruled by Antarctic fur seals, and have time to observe wallowing elephant seals.

There are a number of outstanding landing sites here. A few trips attempt Point Wild, on Elephant Island, to pay homage to the 22 men – Frank Wild among them – stranded here for four months in 1916 until Ernest Shackleton came to the rescue. More likely stops include: Penguin

Iceberg ahoy: Zodiacs – rigid-hulled inflatables – provide the best way of getting out amid the ice

My best day

I love to sit on a particular rock high above Paradise Bay. It's one of my favourite places. One day the sun was shining and the view was exceptionally breathtaking, even by Antarctic standards. Immediately below me, two humpback whales cruised past a cluster of crabeater seals, fast asleep on a piece of floating ice. Beyond them, a huge white-and-blue glacier was calving, the lightning cracks and thunderous booms echoing around the bay. And behind me, on a veritable mountain of weathered rocks, there was an entirely different world of snowy sheathbills, giant petrels, kelp gulls and Antarctic shags. I remember trying to take it all in and thinking: it doesn't get much better than this.

After you: A trio of gentoos teeters on the ice, preparing to take the plunge

Right: Weddell seals live further south than any other mammal; Antarctic ice is never dull; Hope Bay is home to one of world's largest adélie colonies

Island, which looks rather like the surface of the moon and is home to nesting chinstrap penguins and southern giant petrels; Aitcho Islands, for their nesting chinstrap and gentoo penguins, wallowing southern elephant seals and scattered whale bones; Half Moon Island, a small crescent-shaped island with breeding chinstrap penguins, Antarctic shags, Wilson's storm petrels, snowy sheathbills, sub-Antarctic skuas and other seabirds; Yankee Harbor on Greenwich Island, well-known for its breeding gentoo penguins and many ill-tempered Antarctic fur seals; and Hannah Point on Livingston Island, which has a bit of everything (it also offers one of the best chances of seeing macaroni penguins).

A particular highlight is Deception Island, a collapsed volcanic cone whose centre is accessible by ship through a narrow opening, called Neptune's Bellows, in the volcano's walls. Sailing into its flooded caldera is an experience in itself. Apart from the spectacular volcanic scenery, this ring-shaped island is jam-packed with chinstrap penguins, has a thriving colony of Antarctic fur seals, and is home to an old Norwegian whaling station and an abandoned British Antarctic Survey base. It may even be possible to take a dip in some hot thermal waters inside.

A visit to an active research station, such as the Polish Arctowski or Brazilian Ferraz, is another possibility. There are many cutting-edge science projects in the South Shetlands, including the longest-running penguin project in the world.

Antarctic Peninsula

Leaving the South Shetland Islands, the ship sails across Bransfield Strait towards the northern end of the Antarctic Peninsula. Resembling a bent arm, pointing vaguely north-east, this is a land of broad straits, narrow channels, sweeping bays, mountainous islands and towering tabular icebergs.

While much of the vast and stark Antarctic Continent – an area greater than the United States and Mexico combined – suffers a relative dearth of animal life, brutally cold temperatures as low as -89°C (-128°F), biting winds and many weeks of permanent winter darkness, by contrast the Antarctic Peninsula offers a profusion of wildlife and a much milder climate.

A tour here is complete with a plethora of penguins (rookeries of gentoo, chinstrap and adélie – and you might even see a juvenile emperor penguin), close encounters with whales and seals, more ice and breathtaking scenery than it's possible to imagine and at least one visit to a working scientific station. There are also plenty of opportunities to see Antarctic shags, kelp gulls, Antarctic terns, south polar and sub-Antarctic skuas, snowy sheathbills, even snow petrels, and many other special birds.

The seals you are most likely to see on and around the Peninsula are Weddell, crabeater and leopard. The Weddell seal has the most southerly distribution of any mammal and is common here; it has a remarkable range of vocalisations that can be heard both above and below the ice. The

crabeater seal is believed to be the world's most abundant pinniped (estimates vary but there are probably 10-15 million of them); they are found mainly far south on the Antarctic pack ice. With its unmistakable reptilian-shaped head, the fearsome leopard seal is another familiar sight around the Peninsula; it is usually seen alone, resting on ice or hunting near penguin rookeries.

The Peninsula is home to large numbers of whales. Three species are seen regularly – humpback, Antarctic minke and orca – and many people experience close encounters with at least one of them from the Zodiacs. Humpbacks are extremely common in some areas and it's not unusual to see 100 or more in a single day.

Possible stops (depending on weather and ice conditions) include: Hope Bay, which is home to one of the largest colonies of adélie penguins in the world as well as the friendly Argentine base, Esperanza; Paulet Island, surrounded by massive icebergs calved from the Larsen Ice Shelf and home to another massive adélie penguin colony; Port Lockroy, one of the most-visited sites in Antarctica, with its gentoo penguins, whale bones, a British base and a post office run by the UK Antarctic Heritage Trust (the only chance to send postcards home); Paradise Bay, surrounded by wild mountains, filled with myriad ice floes and majestic icebergs, and often described as one of the most beautiful natural harbours in the world; Petermann Island, a gorgeous snow-covered island with tobogganing adélie penguins, as well

"The great thing about visiting this place at the bottom of the world – perhaps the ultimate wilderness destination – is that it is easy"

as the southernmost breeding colony of gentoos; and the famous Lemaire Channel, a spectacularly beautiful seven-mile long ice-choked waterway, sandwiched between Booth Island and the mainland, complete with resting seals and lots of birds.

Then it's back across the Drake, with a short stop at Cape Horn (weather permitting) to marvel at one of the most famous landmarks in the world and to look for the Peale's dolphins and myriad seabirds that seem to hang around there with wonderful regularity. Then, before you know it, you're back in Ushuaia.

A comfortable adventure

Marco Polo had an interesting theory about adventures: 'An adventure is misery and discomfort' he said, 'relived in the safety of reminiscence'. Unfortunately, he never had the opportunity to travel on an Antarctic expedition cruise ship.

The greatest thing about visiting this place at the bottom of the world – perhaps the ultimate wildlife and wilderness

Below: The Antarctic ice provides as many photo opportunities as the resident wildlife

destination – is that it's easy. Most of the expedition cruise ships plying Antarctic waters are like comfortable hotels, with almost as many staff as guests, teams of international experts on everything from polar exploration to seabirds, mind-bogglingly spectacular views out of every window, superb international cuisine, and a range of facilities including well-stocked libraries and theatre-style auditoria.

A typical day – if, indeed, there is a typical day – begins with a friendly wake-up call and breakfast. The morning might begin with an informative lecture, or a chance to watch as the ship picks its way through the polar ice. Then comes the call to get ready – to don the brightly coloured Antarctic jackets, trousers and Wellington boots – for the first shore landing of the day.

Every ship carries a fleet of sturdy Zodiacs (rigid-hulled inflatable boats) to transfer expedition staff and passengers quickly and safely to otherwise inaccessible wildlife, historical or scientific sites. At first, many people worry about getting in and out of the Zodiacs with their cameras and pride intact. But, after the first – often hilarious – attempts at stepping ashore gracefully, it soon becomes second nature. Many people stay ashore for the maximum time allowed – typically from one to three hours depending on the day's itinerary – but the Zodiacs make good water-taxis and ferry people backwards and forwards according to demand.

Lunch will frequently be interrupted by ever-changing scenery and spectacular wildlife spied through the portholes, while the ship cruises to the next venue. Few holidays offer such awe-inspiring and ever-changing scenery over a single meal. Then comes another call to get ready. It might be for a second shore landing at a different site, or for a Zodiac cruise through beautiful ice scenery, past seals and

SPECIES CHECKLIST

- Leopard seal
- Crabeater seal
- Weddell seal
- Southern elephant seal
- Antarctic fur seal
- Humpback whale
- Antarctic minke whale
- Orca
- Southern right whale
- Fin whale
- Peale's dolphin
- Hourglass dolphin
- Gentoo penguin
- Adélie penguin
- Chinstrap penguin
- Macaroni penguin
- Wandering albatross
- Northern royal albatross
- Southern royal albatross
- Black-browed albatross
- Grey-headed albatross
- Light-mantled sooty albatross
- Southern giant petrel
- Northern giant petrel
- Cape petrel
- Antarctic petrel
- Snow petrel
- Antarctic prion
... and many more

Smile!: A leopard seal has a strangely reptilian head

Need to know

WHEN TO GO

The Antarctic season runs from **November to mid-March** (the southern spring and summer) and each month has its special highlights. November is best for ice, pristine snow and **courting penguins**. December and January are warmer, with longer hours of daylight, penguins feeding their chicks and better whale-watching; the receding ice also opens up new channels for exploration. February and early March are best for **whale-watching**, but the penguin rookeries have quietened down and much of the snow has melted or turned to mud. During the Antarctic summer, **temperatures** at the Antarctic Peninsula range from about -10°C (14°F) to 6°C (43°F) but usually hover just above zero.

HOW TO DO IT

Most **expedition cruise ships** leave Ushuaia, southern Argentina, for the South Shetland Islands and the Antarctic Peninsula. Trips typically last 9-14 nights. Longer trips include the Falkland Islands and South Georgia. The notorious sail across the **Drake Passage** takes about two days and can be tough but is swiftly forgotten as soon as you reach the protected waterways near the continent. Once there, expect two or three landings or Zodiac cruises every day (depending on the size of ship and the weather).

The largest ships offer cheaper tours but have so many passengers they need to operate a shift system (**no more than 100 people are allowed on shore at one time**), which means that each passenger has considerably fewer (and shorter) landings. Some are so large than no one goes ashore – they are for cruising only. Large ships are also likely to cause more disruption and could pose a serious threat to passenger safety, given

limited resources available in an emergency. The smallest ships offer more space ashore, but take longer to cross the Drake and give a rougher ride. Ships carrying about 100 passengers are the perfect compromise.

Alternatively, it is possible to **fly from Punta Arenas** in southern Chile to King George Island, in the South Shetlands, for a day trip or to join a ship already there. Admittedly, you avoid the sea crossing, but it's expensive and you miss out on the real adventure.

penguins resting on ice floes, or among feeding whales.

In the evening, there may be another shore landing or Zodiac cruise, a lecture in the auditorium, or you may choose to spend a few more exhilarating hours on deck before forcing yourself to turn in for the night. One of the problems with visiting the Antarctic in mid-summer is the long hours of daylight. Even after a full day of

intrepid adventure, with the ship well on its way to the next breathtaking destination, you daren't sleep for fear of missing something. You want to be on deck, or on the bridge, to glimpse just one more iceberg, one more Antarctic seal or one more whale, or to take just one more spectacular photograph.

There is only one solution – stay up all night and then sleep when you get home.

Avian overload: Every morning in winter, tens of thousands of snow geese lift off simultaneously from the Bosque Refuge

Rising with the BIRDS

New Mexico: Bosque del Apache National Wildlife Refuge

As the sun peeps above the horizon, and the morning mist burns orange, unimaginable numbers of snow geese erupt in an explosion of wings

The experience

What? A true wildlife spectacle, guaranteed to lift your soul

Where? A watery oasis packed with wildlife, on the edge of the Chihuahuan Desert, New Mexico, USA

How? Fly to Albuquerque and hire a car

Bosque del Apache is one of the best birding spots in North America, a 90-square-mile refuge of floodplain, irrigated farms, wetlands, grasslands and mountain foothills, straddling the Rio Grande. It is also the place to go for one of the greatest wildlife spectacles on the planet.

It doesn't last long – maybe ten seconds for the best part – but it's up there with any other wildlife spectacle you'd care to mention, and people travel from all over the world specially to see it.

In most years the focal point is the Flight Deck – a wooden observation platform built on stilts over the main lake. This overlooks a major roost for snow geese and Ross's geese; on a good day, there are tens of thousands of them milling around on the water, calling incessantly to each other. They are joined in the early hours, in the

"The sound of their wing-beats is worth the trip alone: the roar was almost deafening – like a goal-scoring cheer at a football match"

My best day

I'd seen so many photographs of Bosque over the years that I could close my eyes and imagine that classic scene – a trillion geese launching themselves from an extraordinary orange mist. To be honest, my first visit wasn't as good as I'd been imagining, but I persevered and now that I've witnessed the spectacle first-hand I can see what all the fuss is about. I remember three things about the best morning: it was bitterly cold; there was no warning before blast-off (one moment the birds were milling around on the lake and the next they were all in the air); and the noise was as impressive as the sight itself.

dark, by many more geese that roosted in other parts of the refuge overnight.

Photographers and bird watchers gather here every winter morning before dawn, waiting in muffled silence for the great spectacle, dubbed 'liftoff'. On a good day, just as the sun peeks above the hills behind the lake and burns through the ground fog, the whole landscape turns orange and it looks as if the birds are in a huge blaze.

With or without this 'fire-in-the-mist', there is a subtle trigger and, suddenly, unimaginable numbers of geese take to the air en masse in front of the rising sun. They fly in layers, low over the Flight Deck, frantically honking as they head out to feed in their favourite fields. A friend once enthused that the sound of their wing-beats alone was worth the trip (he said the roar of the birds taking flight was almost deafening – like a goal-scoring cheer at a football match). It's so thrilling and exhilarating it certainly 'wows' you out of your worries.

Within about ten seconds, virtually all the tens of thousands of geese are airborne and then the lake is empty. Empty of geese, at least. It is also a hotspot for sandhill cranes (Bosque is a critical refuge for them – supporting as many as 16,000 at one time) and they gradually drift away in smaller groups after the geese have done their thing.

Once the early morning spectacle is over, there is plenty of other wildlife-watching to enjoy until the geese and cranes return for the night. However, the honking of the geese and the guttural call of cranes are never far away, and you can see them around the refuge all day long: little groups in flight, or feeding in the surrounding fields.

But Bosque is also home to vast numbers of other birds, in terms of both numbers (up to 140,000 ducks and geese of many different species at any one time) and variety (no fewer than 377 bird species have been recorded altogether).

There is a fabulous 12-mile one-way Loop Road, with plenty of places to stop, a number of wooden observation decks and lots of short walking trails (from 1.5 to 10 miles). Slowly driving around the Loop Road is the best way to view Bosque's wildlife. It passes close to foraging areas of cranes and geese, ponds packed with green-winged teal, ring-necked ducks, buffleheads, pintails and other wildfowl, hotspots for hawks and eagles (bald eagles are often perched near the Flight Deck

SPECIES CHECKLIST

- Snow goose
- Ross's goose
- Sandhill crane
- White-crowned sparrow
- Roadrunner
- Green-winged teal
- Ring-necked duck
- Bufflehead
- Pintail
- Ruddy duck
- Common merganser
- Bald eagle
- Cooper's hawk
- Harrier hawk
- Red-tailed hawk
- Yellow-headed blackbird
- American goldfinch
- Lesser goldfinch
- Rock wren
- Sage sparrow
- Savannah sparrow
- Ruby-crowned kinglet
- Mountain lion
- Elk
- Coyote
- Mule deer
- Porcupine
- Muskrat
- Beaver
- Jackrabbit
- Desert cottontail
- Rock squirrel
- Hispid cotton rat
  ...and many more

and on trees along Marsh Loop), and good places to see everything from roadrunners to ruby-crowned kinglets. The wildlife here is accustomed to cars and, if you resist the temptation to get out, your vehicle will make an excellent hide enabling you to observe everything surprisingly closely.

I've encountered more coyotes in Bosque than anywhere else in North America, too. They are frequently seen during winter on the Farm Loop

The cranes remain: Bosque del Apache is a critical refuge for up to 16,000 sandhill cranes

Left: While bird-watching at the reserve, look out for coyote, too

Need to know

WHEN TO GO

The big spectacle takes place in winter, with the greatest number of geese and cranes occurring from **early December to mid-February**. However, it's a little bit hit-and-miss and has certainly been less predictable in recent years. The specific location of 'liftoff' may also vary from day to day.

Temperatures are usually pleasant during the day, but it can be freezing cold before dawn (down to -15°C [5°F] when I was there one January). The **Festival of the Cranes**, which celebrates the return of the cranes with guided tours, exhibits and workshops, is held every year in November.

The diversity of birds in Bosque is also high during **spring** (especially late April-early May) and **autumn**, when you can see northern harriers, American avocets, northern orioles, black-chinned hummingbirds and more. **Summer is hot, and much quieter**, but is good for a number of species, including abundant black-chinned hummingbirds, blue grosbeaks, black phoebes and wild turkeys; take insect repellant if you're visiting at this time.

HOW TO DO IT

Fly to Albuquerque, in New Mexico, and then drive to Bosque – it takes less than two hours and, ideally, you need a car to get around once there. Hotels and guesthouses are available in Socorro (20 miles away) and the small town of San Antonio (10 miles). There are also two campsites and RV parks within striking distance of the refuge.

The **Loop Road** is open daily for driving, walking and (seasonally) cycling, from one hour before sunrise to one hour after sunset. It's a mixture of refuge tracks and gravel. The road starts near the **Visitor Centre**, which is an excellent source of information on everything from bird counts to unusual recent sightings; in winter, around the centre itself is good for rock squirrels, hispid cotton rats and desert cottontails, as well as Cooper's hawks and roadrunners. You do have to **get up early** to see the snow goose spectacle: lie in and you will miss it.

(another small section of the Loop Road), usually hanging around the geese. Also look out for beavers and muskrats in the canals and ponds, as well as mule deer and porcupines on the sides of the roads.

As the day draws to a close, late in the afternoon, it's time to revisit the Flight Deck to watch the return of all the geese and cranes. Their reappearance at the lake, to roost for the night, isn't as dramatic as their early morning departure.

But watching them streaking the sky in long wobbly skeins, as the sun drops below the horizon, is truly a glorious sight.

Some time in late February or March, the geese leave Bosque and fly north. Travelling at high altitude, in very large, noisy flocks, they migrate several thousand miles to breed on the high Arctic tundra of Alaska, Canada and even north-east Russia. They return the following November, and the daily spectacle starts all over again.

Shouting from the treetops: A proboscis monkey shows off its distinctive pot belly and pendulous nose

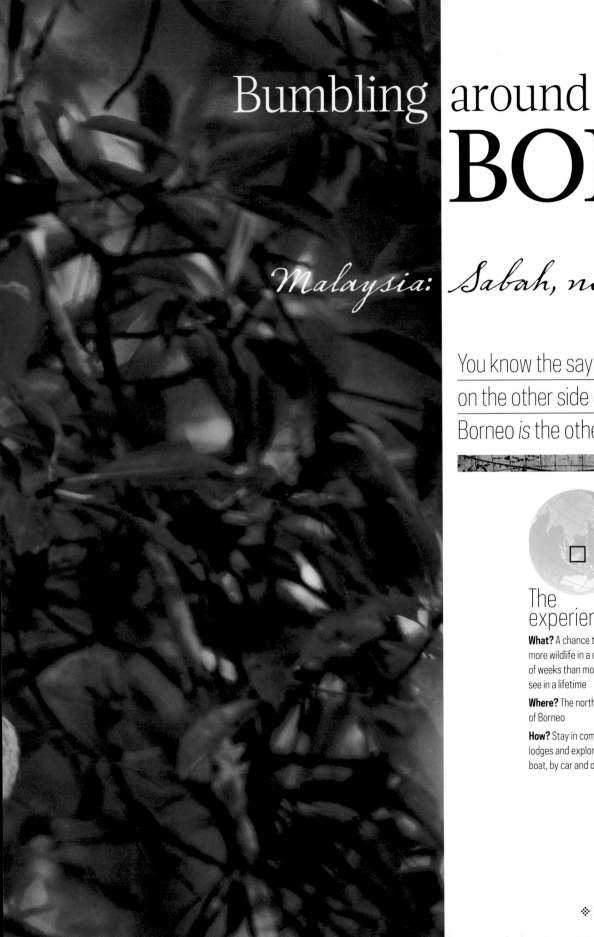

Bumbling around
BORNEO

Malaysia: *Sabah, northern Borneo*

You know the saying "the grass is always greener on the other side of the fence"? Well, northern Borneo *is* the other side of the fence

The experience

What? A chance to see more wildlife in a couple of weeks than most people see in a lifetime

Where? The northern tip of Borneo

How? Stay in comfortable lodges and explore by boat, by car and on foot

The island of Borneo is divided between three different countries: Indonesia (which owns Kalimantan), Brunei (one of the smallest countries in the world) and Malaysia (which owns Sarawak and Sabah). I particularly like Sabah, because it includes many of the most accessible wildlife-rich regions of the island.

With crystal-clear turquoise seas, gorgeous white-sand tropical islands, rugged mountain ranges and dense tropical rainforest – not to mention some 10,000 species of flowering plants, 900 species of butterfly, 520 species of bird and nearly 200 species of mammal – it's hard to know where to begin with this land of milk and honey. A true biodiversity hotspot, Sabah is full to the brim with beauty and wildlife.

And all this despite vast swathes of what was once tropical rainforest being cleared

Top left: The animal most people think of when they think of Borneo: an orang utan

Top right: A western tarsier in Danum Valley

Above: A mammalian pine cone (otherwise known as a pangolin)

Opposite: The Bornean pygmy elephant is the world's smallest elephant (it's a sub-species of the Asian elephant)

to make way for mile upon mile of palm oil plantations – the single most immediate threat to the greatest number of species on the planet. When the forests go, so do most of the native plants and animals. In a place like Borneo, that means a heck of a lot of different species.

But still there are orangutans (Borneo and Sumatra are the only places to see these huge, intelligent apes), proboscis monkeys, Müller's Bornean gibbons (waking up to their distinctive songs ringing through the treetops is one of the great Bornean experiences), Sumatran rhinos, Bornean pygmy elephants (a diminutive race of Asian elephant), Malaysian sun bears, clouded leopards, mouse deer, giant flying squirrels, rhinoceros hornbills, edible-nest swiftlets, and much, much more.

There are also lots of easily overlooked (but equally enthralling) creatures: worms as long as your arm, frogs the size of your fingernail, fish that jump (you can see mudskippers skipping about in mangrove

swamps all over Sabah), and the largest and sometimes smelliest flowers in the world.

There are many splendid wildlife places to visit, but here are a few of my favourites:

Kinabalu National Park

The focal point of beautiful Kinabalu National Park, Malaysia's first World Heritage site, is Mount Kinabalu. This peak reaches a height of 13,435 feet and is the tallest mountain between the Himalayas and New Guinea.

But the area is just as well known for its unbelievably rich and luxuriant plant life. It is teeming with orchids (1,200 species at the last count), some of the largest carnivorous pitcher plants in the world, and more than 600 fern species, to name just a few. One of the jewels in its crown is *Rafflesia*, the largest single bloom of any flowering plant in the world. Its flower, which is bright red with creamy-white spots, can grow up to three feet across and smells horrible – like rotting flesh.

Kinabalu is also outstanding for birds: 326 species, no less, including 18 Bornean endemics. Specialities include the Kinabalu serpent eagle, Kinabalu friendly warbler, green magpie, crimson-breasted wood partridge and Bornean mountain whistler.

There are loads of mammals, too, including two endemic shrews and several flying squirrels. No fewer than 133 species have been recorded here, though most of them keep themselves to themselves. Look out for weird and wonderful invertebrates as well, such as the endemic Kinabalu giant red leech and the Kinabalu giant earthworm. The streams around the park HQ are great for amphibians and reptiles – night walks reveal everything from Kinabalu horned frogs to green mountain agamas and Kinabalu forest geckos.

There is a canopy walkway and there are lots of nature trails on the lower slopes. Or you can hike to the top of Mount Kinabalu itself (allow two days; hire porters and guides at the park headquarters).

SPECIES CHECKLIST

- Bornean orangutan
- Proboscis monkey
- Crab-eating macaque
- Pig-tailed macaque
- Grey leaf monkey (Hose's langur)
- Red leaf monkey (maroon langur)
- Silvered langur
- Müller's Bornean gibbon
- Slow loris
- Western tarsier
- Giant squirrel
- Leopard cat
- Oriental small-clawed otter
- Bornean pygmy elephant
- Banteng
- Bearded pig
- Wrinkle-lipped bat
- Black-nest swiftlet
- White-nest swiftlet
- Wrinkled hornbill
- Rhinoceros hornbill
- Wreathed hornbill
- Oriental pied hornbill
- Helmeted hornbill
- Kinabalu serpent eagle
- Kinabalu friendly warbler
- Sunda ground cuckoo
- Raffles's malkoha
- Water monitor lizard
- Green turtle
- Hawksbill turtle
- Whitetip reef shark
- Grey reef shark
- Scalloped hammerhead shark
- Leopard shark
- Mudskipper
- *Rafflesia*
- Pitcher plant

… and many more

> # "Every evening one million swiftlets return to the cave and hundreds of thousands of bats swarm out – it looks as if the walls are spinning"

Kinabatangan Wildlife Sanctuary

The Kinabatangan is the longest river in Sabah. As it approaches the sea, in the north-eastern corner of the state, it forms a vast floodplain ecosystem of almost unparalleled richness. It is one of South-East Asia's most important rainforests.

This is a great location for primates, with ten different species living here. In particular, it is one of the best places in Sabah to see wild orangutans. Look for large trees in fruit along the river, where an orang or two might have briefly settled.

It is also one of the best places to see proboscis monkeys, which are best spotted from a boat – groups of up to 30 feed in riverside trees; if you are lucky, you may see them diving into the water. Crab-eating and pig-tailed macaques, Bornean gibbons, silvered langurs and grey leaf monkeys are commonly seen in Kinabatangan, too.

Bornean pygmy elephants are seen more often here than anywhere else in Sabah, especially at well-known crossing points on the river. Rarer mammalian sightings include Malaysian sun bears, flat-headed cats and clouded leopards.

Bird watching is spectacular along the Kinabatangan, with wrinkled, rhinoceros and helmeted hornbills, endangered Sunda ground cuckoos, Raffles's malkohas (a kind of cuckoo) and red-crowned barbets among the species to look out for.

It's also fantastic for snakes – you can see them coiled up on branches overhanging the river; look out for yellow-ringed cat snakes, Wagler's pit vipers and young reticulated pythons, in particular.

The sanctuary is best explored by boat. There are also some good viewing platforms and rainforest boardwalks.

Sepilok Orangutan Sanctuary

Situated in the Kabili-Sepilok Forest Reserve, outside Sandakan, this is one of the better orangutan rehabilitation centres in Borneo. It works as a kind of hospital and re-training ground for orangs confiscated from captivity, orphaned by hunting or displaced by forest clearance. Twice-daily feeding sessions usually attract a number of habituated individuals to a platform in the forest, so sightings are relatively easy, though not guaranteed.

There are also guided walks through the reserve, and these offer the chance to see more orangs along the boardwalks and trails. They have all been nursed back to health and taught the skills essential to survive in the jungle. You might also see Bornean gibbons, red leaf monkeys, pig-tailed macaques and flying squirrels (probably Hose's pygmy) along the way.

Gomantong Caves

Between Sepilok and Kinabatangan are the Gomantong Caves. The surrounding reserve is home to orangutans, bearded pigs, mouse deer and other wildlife, but this intricate cave system is most famous for its bats and swiftlets.

For centuries, the caves have been renowned for their valuable swiftlet nests, which are still harvested to make the Chinese delicacy, bird's nest soup. Under licence, twice a year (February to April and July to September) locals use rattan ladders, ropes and bamboo poles to climb as high as 300 feet to the roof of the cave to collect the nests. There are two species – white-nest (which make the most valuable nests) and black-nest swiftlets.

The cave system is also home to huge numbers of bats. Every evening, just as one million swiftlets are making their way back for the night, hundreds of thousands of mainly wrinkle-lipped bats (and a few other species) swarm out like clouds of smoke. There is such a gargantuan swirling

Below: A silvered langur at Labuk Bay

Perfect perch: Bird watching from a canopy walkway in Danum Valley

Opposite: Gomantong is home to a million swiftlets and hundreds of thousands of bats

My best day

One of the many highlights of bumbling around Borneo was the first time I ever saw a proboscis monkey, in Labuk Bay. This rather ridiculous-looking creature is my favourite primate, up there with mountain gorillas and ahead of orangutans. How can you not like an animal with a pot belly and a red, pendulous nose? It even has a ready-made cushion – a thickened, hairless patch of skin on its backside – for that extra-special comfort when sitting down. The male is particularly impressive, with a jet-black scrotum and a bright-red penis (and what seems like a permanent erection). It was the animal itself, rather than a particular encounter, that made my day.

mass of birds and bats that, from inside, it looks as if the walls are spinning. Visit at sunset to witness the spectacle at its best, and look out for bat hawks, peregrines and buffy fish owls picking off the caves' inhabitants from the outside.

There are two trails leading into different parts of the cave system. One takes about five hours of more serious caving; the other involves nothing more than a short stroll. The entire floor is covered with guano (which, in turn, is covered with an incalculable number of cockroaches and everything from harmless dung beetles to highly venomous centipedes) so the easier trail follows a wooden walkway circling the interior. Don't forget to wear a hat!

Danum Valley Conservation Area

A wonderful rainforest reserve in central Sabah, Danum Valley is one of the best remaining tracts of primary lowland rainforest in Borneo and one of the island's top wildlife destinations.

It is a good place to see wild orangutans (there are believed to be about 500 of the apes in the conservation area) and is home to nine other primate species. It is particularly outstanding for Bornean gibbons and red leaf monkeys. Night walks and drives offer the chance to see two other primates – the western tarsier and slow loris – as well as flying squirrels and even leopard cats.

Other mammals you might see while here include Bornean pygmy elephants,

bearded pigs, Bornean red muntjac and mouse deer. And Danum Valley is home to such mouth-watering elusives and rarities as Sumatran rhinos, Malaysian sun bears, clouded leopards and flat-headed cats – unfortunately, while you may well find signs of their presence, don't expect to see them unless you are incredibly lucky.

Danum Valley is also the place to come for hornbills as it hosts all of Borneo's eight species (rhinoceros, wrinkled and wreathed are particularly evident). Altogether, 340 bird species have been recorded here, including blue-headed pitta, Bornean bristlehead, frogmouth and coucal owl.

There are some lovely trails through the forest and a 1,000-foot-long, 90-feet-high canopy walkway. Early morning is best for

"The sea turtles of Sipadan seem completely unperturbed by people in the water – it's not uncommon to see 30 in one dive or snorkel"

seeing some of the more elusive mammals, while nocturnal jungle walks, drives and boat safaris can be productive.

Pulau Sipadan

Right on the border with the Philippines, in the Celebes Sea, Sipadan is a pile of living coral sitting on top of an extinct volcano. What you see from the surface is a tiny 30-acre mop of rainforest surrounded by a narrow strip of white sand. The ultimate tropical island – it makes you want to sing and dance – it is so small it takes no more than 20-30 minutes to stroll all the way round. And nowhere is it more than the height of a man above sea level.

Sipadan is full to overflowing with marine life. Less than 70 feet from the beach is a stunning reef wall that plunges to depths of more than 2,000 feet. It is reputed to offer the best shore diving and snorkelling anywhere in the world, though the currents can be brutally strong (most of the dives are for experienced divers only). There are also many excellent dive sites accessible by boat, no more than ten minutes away.

It is best known for its sea turtles; there are huge numbers of green turtles, which seem completely unperturbed by people in the water, as well as smaller numbers of hawksbill turtles. They are pretty much everywhere – it is not uncommon to see 20-30 turtles in a single dive or snorkel – and close encounters are virtually guaranteed.

Sipadan can also be excellent for sharks – one species or another is seen almost every time you get in the water. The best places for encounters with them are places where the currents tend to be strongest, such as Barracuda Point and South Point.

Whitetip reef sharks are seen on virtually every dive and snorkel; try walking through the shallows at first light to see the juveniles patrolling with young blacktip reef sharks (and keep your eyes peeled for large water monitors wandering along the beach). Grey reef sharks and scalloped hammerheads are also common, although they tend to be a little deeper. Various other species turn up from time to time, including leopard, thresher and whale sharks.

Other underwater treasures to look out for include manta, eagle and blue-spotted rays, huge schools of jack, big-eye trevally and barracuda, and giant clams. The reef itself is teeming with a range of outrageously colourful fish.

Labuk Bay Proboscis Monkey Sanctuary

This private reserve is in the heart of the mangrove forests of Semawang, within a palm oil estate. Although it is all rather artificial, with twice-daily feeding times at the centre, it is an excellent place to see and photograph proboscis monkeys close-up.

There are also red leaf monkeys and silvered langurs here, both of which are habituated. It's a good place for bird watching, with oriental pied hornbills

Right: Hatchlings at Turtle Island National Park make their bid for the sea

Below: You're likely to see a whitetip reef shark every time you get in the water at Sipadan

Need to know

WHEN TO GO

The **dry season** is from **May to October**, although it is not always dry. **The wet is from November to April** (November to January tends to be wettest) although it is not always wet. The best time to go varies, depending on what you most want to see and where, but there are wildlife watching opportunities year-round. **Sea turtles** lay their eggs at any time, but especially during the dry season, with a peak in June.

On **Sipadan**, the best diving is during the north-east monsoon, from **July to September**, which is also the busiest period. The best time for scalloped hammerheads, manta rays and whale sharks is late November to January (coinciding with the worst visibility and lowest temperatures).

HOW TO DO IT

Fly to **Kuala Lumpur** for connecting flights to various cities in Sabah, or to **Singapore** to connect to Sabah's capital, **Kota Kinabalu**. It's easy to hire a car or, alternatively, there are flights and air-conditioned buses connecting major towns and cities within the state. Use **river boats** to reach more remote areas.

A wide **range of hotels, jungle lodges, chalets, longhouses and mountain huts** offers accommodation throughout the region, including in many of the best wildlife areas. Some have their **own viewing platforms**, trails and boardwalks at wildlife hotspots along rivers or in the rainforest.

A few of the best lodges include: Sutera Sanctuary Lodge, for **Kinabalu** (this is the only accommodation inside the park, but there is a big choice of other hotels, lodges and cabins outside); Sukau River Lodge, Nature Lodge Kinabatangan, Kinabatangan Riverside Lodge and Sukau Rainforest Lodge, for **Kinabatangan**; Sepilok Nature Resort and Sepilok Jungle Resort, for **Sepilok Orangutan Sanctuary**; Nipah Lodge for **Labuk Bay**; and Borneo Rainforest Lodge or Danum Valley Field Centre for **Danum Valley**. There is simple accommodation for tourists at the park headquarters on Selingan, for **Turtle Island**.

No one is allowed to stay overnight on **Sipadan**. Instead, there is a choice of hotels and resorts on neighbouring Mabul and Kapalai islands or, a little further away, on Mataking and in the small port of Semporna.

a bit of a speciality, and there are night tours to see flying squirrels, fireflies and myriad other wildlife.

Turtle Island National Park

Turtle Island Park, in the Sulu Sea off the north-eastern coast of Sabah, comprises three beautiful islands – Selingan, Bakungan Kecil and Gulisan. This is *the* place to come to learn about green and hawksbill turtles, and to see them nesting.

You have to stay overnight on Selingan, the largest of the islands, to join rangers on turtle patrol. Watch as they check the beaches for females coming ashore to lay their eggs in the sand, and see them collect the valuable clutches for safe-keeping near the park headquarters.

They go to the turtle hatchery, which has hundreds of artificial turtle nests in neat rows across the sand. Each nest is labelled, with a date and the number of eggs inside, and protected with a circle of plastic mesh roughly the size of a bucket.

It is also possible to watch turtle hatchlings being released at the back of the beach. They need a run-up before entering the sea, to help them get their bearings, then they race straight into the surf and swim away as if they've been doing it their whole lives. Watching them is a real privilege, a truly magical experience.

California dreaming: After a hearty lunch, a Monterey sea otter folds its arms and prepares for a nap

Lunching with the SEA OTTERS

California: Monterey

Wildlife and concrete are rarely a happy mix – but I've never had a bad week wildlife-watching in this delightful Californian coastal town

The experience

What? Watching sea otters and other coastal Californian wildlife while eating a leisurely lunch in a restaurant by the sea

Where? The city of Monterey, 100 miles south of San Francisco

How? Book a table by the window

I've spent a surprising amount of time nature-watching in towns and cities around the world: polar bears from my hotel in Churchill, northern Canada; southern right whales from Cape Town's busy Victoria & Alfred Waterfront; and thousands of migrating birds from a bar in Gibraltar. I'll never forget braving horrendous traffic for several hours to get to one of the world's largest turtle-nesting beaches on the outskirts of Karachi, Pakistan. And I spent a happy day in the bustling Indian city of Guwahati, Assam, watching Ganges river dolphins in the Brahmaputra River.

But my favourite urban jungle for watching wildlife is Monterey, in central California. It may not be as thrilling as ice-diving, wilderness camping or mountain trekking, but it has its own special rewards. And it's easy.

My best day

I'll never forget my first visit to Monterey, because it was the beginning of a long and happy friendship (if you can have a friendship with a place). I drove from San Francisco, stopping off at Año Nuevo for a pleasant morning with the elephant seals, and arrived in Monterey in time for lunch on Fisherman's Wharf (the first of many over the years). I remember counting no fewer than seven different sea otters from the restaurant window. Then I joined an afternoon whale-watch trip and saw six different cetacean species, including a blue whale and a huge school of northern rightwhale dolphins. I was supposed to be continuing to Santa Cruz that night, but made my excuses and stayed in Monterey instead.

All you have to do is to pick one of many restaurants along Fisherman's Wharf, a wooden pier standing on stilts in the middle of the harbour, and ask for a table overlooking the water. The Wharf is a tourist trap at heart but you'll see more wildlife here in a couple of hours, between mouthfuls of Caesar salad and clam chowder, than you'll see by trudging around many well-known national parks.

Brown pelicans peer inquisitively through the windows, there are myriad other seabirds, waterfowl and waders around the marina, harbour seals are fast asleep on many of the rocks, and I've even seen endangered northern elephant seals coming in for a closer look.

Admittedly, it can be a little noisy at times – thanks to the contorted gatherings of California sea lions lounging around beneath the pier, barking incessantly. Sometimes, they can be so animated and argumentative that, if you're sitting too close to their haul-outs, you have to shout to be heard above the uproar. But they are such charismatic animals and so

entertaining to watch that they're never short of an admiring audience. Look for an excited gaggle of tourists peering over the boardwalk towards the sea and the chances are you'll find an excited gaggle of California sea lions peering back.

Best of all, sea otters are on the menu, too. Not in the 'medium-rare sea otter with a side salad' sense, of course, but they're as much a part of eating out in Monterey as chips are a part of eating out in Blackpool. In fact, the Wharf is one of the best places in the world to see these quieter, unshowy marine mammals.

Fisherman's Wharf was once a major fishing pier, focused on sardines. For the first half of the 20th century Monterey lived on the sardine-cannery business; during the 1940s it was the sardine capital of the Western Hemisphere. All those little fish made it a very rich, for a decade at least. But the sardines soon disappeared – partly due to overfishing and also because of a 'boom and bust' cycle that occurs naturally in the Pacific every 30-40 years. They have since made a comeback, which is great news for the many other fish and marine mammals that rely on them.

SPECIES CHECKLIST

- Southern sea otter
- California sea lion
- Harbour seal
- Northern elephant seal
- Blue whale
- Humpback whale
- Grey whale
- Orca
- Dolphins (several species)
- California condor
- Monarch butterfly

...and many more in season

Indeed, Monterey Bay is one of the most fertile and diverse marine environments in the world. Fringed by beaches, tide pools, sand dunes and kelp forests, its centrepiece is a massive underwater canyon comparable in size to the Grand Canyon. Starting just offshore from Moss Landing, about 20 miles north of Monterey, the Monterey Submarine Canyon extends more than 90 miles out to sea and plummets to a depth of over two miles.

The nutrient-rich waters of the Bay are a veritable magnet for whales and dolphins and no fewer than 26 species have been recorded altogether. Although

"Floating past the restaurant windows, the otters are too busy feeding themselves to notice the human diners watching their every move"

Coast with the most: Highly intelligent sea otters compete with California sea lions for the attention of diners on Fisherman's Wharf

Need to know

WHEN TO GO

Sea otters are present in Monterey year-round; most pups are born from January to early March. **California sea lions** and **harbour seals** are present year-round. **Northern elephant seals** are more often seen in summer and autumn; the peak breeding season at Año Nuevo is 15 December to 31 March, but smaller numbers are present year-round. **Monarch butterflies** gather in Pacific Grove mid-October to late February.

Cetacean species vary by season. Dall's and harbour porpoises, and common, Pacific white-sided, Risso's and bottlenose dolphins can be seen year-round. Northern rightwhale dolphins are best seen in September and October. Orcas enter the bay to hunt grey whales in April and May, but can be seen year-round. Late May to early November is good for blue and humpback whales (though humpbacks often appear as early as April, while blues are best in late July and August); fin and minke whales are occasionally seen at this time of year, too. Grey whales are closest to shore on their southern migration (mid-December to mid-April).

HOW TO DO IT

It's simple – just go to Monterey and wander along **Fisherman's Wharf** – or take a packed lunch and watch the otters from a bench.

There are several other local wildlife hotspots, too. Every winter, monarch butterflies gather in enormous clusters on trees in Pacific Grove, just a few miles south of Monterey. The best place is **Monarch Grove Butterfly Sanctuary**, on Ridge Road.

Also worth a visit is **Año Nuevo State Park**, about 60 miles north of Monterey. This is the world's largest mainland northern elephant seal breeding colony. It is also the southernmost breeding site for Steller sea lions (though they are difficult to see) and is home to everything from rare San Francisco garter snakes to red-tailed hawks.

Elsewhere, there are endangered western snowy plovers nesting on the beach at **Salinas River National Wildlife Refuge**; a huge number of birds, Santa Cruz long-toed salamanders and lots of sea otters at **Elkhorn Slough**; and even reintroduced California condors soaring over **Big Sur**.

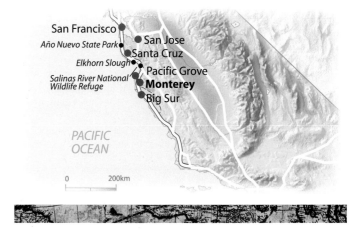

you can't see them easily from Monterey itself, there are boat trips out into the Bay year-round.

There are trips around the harbour too, with sea otters the indubitable stars of the show. There are about 2,700 of them in California, roughly between Año Nuevo and Point Conception; there is also a small colony near San Nicolas Island, off Santa Barbara. They are all descendants of about 50 survivors (after two centuries of commercial hunting for their pelts) discovered near Big Sur in 1938.

Floating past the restaurant windows, they are too busy feeding themselves to

notice the dozens of human diners watching their every move. Sea otters are among the few animals to use tools and actually make use of rocks to break open their hard-shelled prey. They gather molluscs and crustaceans from the seabed, return to the surface, lie on their backs, and then use their chests as tables for smashing the shells before eating the soft-bodied creatures inside.

When they've had their fill, they fold their arms, close their eyes, and take an afternoon nap. All they need is a pair of slippers and a television, and they could almost be human.

The cat's whiskers: The
Pantanal is probably the
world's best place for
close jaguar encounters

Tracking
JAGUARS

Brazil: northern Pantanal

The Amazon gets all the attention, but you see far more wildlife in the Pantanal, a giant wetland which resembles a vast, cage-less zoo

The experience

What? The best-kept secret in South America

Where? A watery wonderland south of the Amazon and east of the Andes

How? Stay in comfortable lodges and explore by 4WD and boat, on horseback and on foot

The Pantanal is the largest continuous wetland on the planet, and it's absolutely stuffed full of wildlife. Three-quarters of this magical place is in Brazil, divided between the states of Mato Grosso and Mato Grosso do Sul; the rest spills over into Bolivia and Paraguay. Covering an area of 77,250 square miles, it is many times bigger than the Okavango Delta in Botswana, and roughly the size of England and Wales combined.

The aquatic heart of South America, it is a seemingly endless mosaic of rivers, lakes, lily-choked ponds, swamps, islands, forest, scrub and wooded savanna (or *cerrado*, as it is known locally). It is a bit like a giant sponge. When the Paraguay, the Cuiabá and several other rivers burst their banks during the rainy season, much of the Pantanal is completely submerged – and

then, during the dry season, most of the water is gradually released. This annual ebb and flow is the pulse of Pantanal life.

Dubbed 'South America's Wild West', it is mind-bogglingly superb for wildlife watching and photography, for four main reasons: the sheer variety of species; the fact that many of them occur in phenomenal numbers; the presence of so many red-letter animals (from jaguars to giant otters – the Pantanal oozes quality as well as quantity); and the relative ease with which they can be found (you do actually get to see most of the local specialities – they're not just names on a list).

With no fewer than 80 species of large mammal (plus lots of bats and small rodents), 650 different birds, 80 species of reptile, at least 50 different amphibians and more than 300 species of fish, there really is masses to see.

High on the list for most visitors is South America's top predator, the jaguar. The Pantanal is probably the best place in the world for close encounters with the largest cat in the Americas.

The sub-species here is twice the size of the individuals living in Central America, and far less elusive. There is one particular spot, on and around the Cuiabá River east of Porto Jofre, where jaguars are seen almost daily during the dry season. They spend a lot of time skulking in the forest and long grass, of course, but they also seem to be fond of the sun, the breeze and the hunting opportunities on riverbanks and, once settled, often spend hours sitting or lying down in the same spot right out in the open.

They are usually alone but, if you're lucky, you may come across a mother with her cubs. The way to do it is to cruise around slowly, in a small boat, checking the riverbanks as you go. Jaguars are strong swimmers, so you may also come across one crossing from one side to the other.

Another must-see species is the giant otter, and the northern Pantanal is a good place for close encounters with this endangered species. It prefers slow-moving rivers with gently sloping banks covered in vegetation, and can be seen at many locations down the length of the Transpantaneira Highway. Some family groups don't seem to be bothered by people and will approach surprisingly close to boats. Consummate performers, they play rough-and-tumble together and 'talk' to one another incessantly.

The mammal you see most often in the Pantanal is the world's largest rodent, the capybara. In fact, for 'most often' read 'all the time'. You can't miss these weird and wonderful animals, with barrel-shaped bodies and slightly webbed feet. They are everywhere – including wandering around the breakfast tables in most lodge gardens.

There are also five species of primate. The largest is the black howler monkey and the dawn roar of the adult male (like something out of *The Blair Witch Project*) is a familiar sound here.

Spotted!: The Pantanal's jaguar is twice the size of the Central American sub-species

SPECIES CHECKLIST

- Jaguar
- Ocelot
- Crab-eating fox
- Giant otter
- Neotropical otter
- South American coati
- Crab-eating raccoon
- Black howler monkey
- Black-striped tufted capuchin
- White-coated titi
- Black-tailed marmoset
- Azara's night monkey
- Giant anteater
- Southern tamandua
- Brazilian tapir
- Collared peccary
- White-lipped peccary
- Capybara
- Marsh deer
- Pampas deer
- South American red brocket deer
- South American brown brocket deer
- Jabiru
- Great potoo
- Common potoo
- Great horned owl
- Hyacinth macaw
- Toco toucan
- Chestnut-eared aracari
- Greater rhea
- Roseate spoonbill
- Grey-necked wood rail
- Yacaré caiman
- Green iguana
- Yellow anaconda
- Green anaconda

… and many, many more

"At least 10 million of them live in the Pantanal – it's reputed to be the largest gathering of crocodiles anywhere in the world"

The drier areas of the cerrado are the most likely spots for giant anteaters, with their long snouts and unbelievably shaggy tails. But if you see an anteater up a tree, it will be another familiar sight, the southern tamandua. Many other mammals are easy to see here and, of course, there are plenty that prefer to keep themselves to themselves. Anyone who glimpses a bush dog, hoary fox, margay, oncilla, Pantanal cat, jaguarundi or puma can count themselves very lucky.

The birds are also a major attraction. Some 650 species are found in the Pantanal and many occur in remarkable numbers. You can see literally thousands in an hour, with herons, egrets, ibises and spoonbills most in evidence. An astonishing number of waders gathers around some of the first bridges on the Transpantaneira Highway in the second half of July and first half of August, in particular. And the region is one of the most important breeding grounds for the jabiru: with a wingspan of over eight feet, this enormous (and noisy) stork is the giant of the Pantanal skies.

Some of the other local specialities include greater rhea, red-legged seriema, several species of pheasant-like guan, great and common potoos, tropical screech-owls, great horned owls, toco toucans and the wonderfully multicoloured chestnut-eared aracaris. It is particularly good for raptors, with several dozen species including snail, white-tailed, pearl and plumbeous kites, long-winged harriers, ospreys, black-chested buzzard eagles, black-collared and zone-tailed hawks, laughing falcons, yellow-headed caracaras, and many more.

Also fantastic for parrots, the Pantanal is home to a sizeable proportion of the world's surviving hyacinth macaws (the largest parrots in the world). You can even see hummingbirds – buff-bellied hermit, gilded sapphire and glittering-bellied emerald among them – in the gardens of many lodges.

The yacaré caiman is by far the most visible reptile. It is one of the smaller crocodilians (although some of the larger individuals can attain a length of almost ten feet) but what it lacks in size it makes up in sheer numbers. Estimates vary considerably, but at least 10 million of them (possibly many more) live in the Pantanal and, in places, they lie side by side on every available riverbank and lake shore. It is reputed to be the largest gathering of crocodiles anywhere in the world.

King of the forest: Jaguars are usually seen alone, but mothers with cubs are sometimes spotted

Right top: There are thought to be 10 million caiman in the Pantanal

Right below: Traffic jams on the Transpantaneira are likely caused by creatures crossing

Snakes are also numerous and the Pantanal is unusual because it has two species of anaconda – yellow and green. Up to 20 feet long and three feet in girth, the green anaconda is one of the biggest snakes in the world.

The area I know best – and adore – is Mato Grosso (the northern Pantanal) and, in particular, the stretch along the Transpantaneira Highway between the small town of Poconé and south as far as Porto Jofre, on the Cuiabá River. You can see most of the Pantanal's wildlife goodies in this region.

The only real exception is the nocturnal maned wolf, which resembles a long-eared

I'll never forget lying in my tent, near the Cuiabá River, listening to the magical sounds of the night. There was the haunting song of a potoo, the oohoo of a horned owl, various excitable frogs, and a cacophony of unidentifiable whistles, hoots, howls and rustlings. Suddenly there was a huge splash and the sound of a serious kerfuffle coming from the river, followed by the unmistakable crash and clatter of something being dragged through the forest undergrowth. I got out of bed, quietly unzipped the tent, and shone my feeble torch into the gloom. There, right in front of me, was a jaguar standing over a huge, freshly killed caiman. I fell asleep, eventually, to the rather disturbing sound of powerful jaws crunching through bone.

fox on stilts and is better seen during the dry season in Mato Grosso do Sul. There are two particular places: Caraça National Park, where the Hospedaria do Colégio Caraça guesthouse (once an old monastery) puts out food on the chapel steps and is visited by maned wolves most nights; and Fazenda San Francisco, 150 miles from Campo Grande on the Miranda River.

The Transpantaneira Highway cuts through the heart of the northern Pantanal. The only road that runs deep into the region (elsewhere you have to travel by boat or small plane), it is linked by a sequence of over 120 (mainly rickety) wooden bridges and offers some of the best roadside wildlife watching in the world. The lakes and ponds on either side are a magnet for birds, capybara and caiman in the dry season; I've seen everything from South American coati and marsh deer to southern tamanduas and even a jaguar running across the road. Traffic is light so the animals treat the highway as their own. There are even colonies of bats roosting under the bridges.

Here are some of my favourite lodges along the Transpantaneira (north to south):

Pousada Piuval

Around 65 miles from Cuiabá, and two miles east of the Transpantaneira Highway, this is the first lodge along the road, and a wildlife haven of grassland, woodland, lakes and ponds. It's a great place for bird-watching, with a good chance of seeing everything from greater rhea and bare-faced curassows to planalto slaty-antshrikes and Mato Grosso antbirds. It is also good for hyacinth macaws, which nest on the property, as well as huge numbers of waterbirds.

Night drives are particularly good here for mammals. You have a better-than-average chance of seeing giant anteater and southern tamandua, and may see puma. This is also one of the best places to see Azara's night monkey.

"When I was last at Porto Jofre, a jaguar suddenly appeared on the river bank right opposite the hotel"

Pousada Araras Ecolodge

With hyacinth macaws and great horned owls visible from the breakfast veranda, and capybara wandering nonchalantly around the garden, this is another great place for a wide variety of wildlife.

There is an elevated wooden boardwalk, which can be good for Brazilian tapir, black-tailed marmosets, Azara's agouti and ocelot. There is also a high tower, offering spectacular views and a chance to get up close and personal with a troop of black howler monkeys that roosts on the top. All sorts of other wildlife is visible along the trails, including South American coatis, nine-banded armadillos and black-striped tufted capuchins.

The wider area is home to giant anteaters and southern tamanduas. Night drives usually encounter both species of brocket deer and crab-eating raccoons, while boat trips on the Clarinho River are good for both giant and neotropical otters.

Right: Giant otters can be seen fishing the waterways

Below: Most jaguar sightings occur near the conjunction between the Cuiabá, Three Brothers and Piquiri rivers

SouthWild Pantanal Lodge (formerly the Pantanal Wildlife Center – Fazenda Santa Tereza)

Located on the banks of the narrow, wildlife-rich Pixaim River, a couple of miles west of the Transpantaneira, the SouthWild Pantanal Lodge is one of the best places for giant otters (which often pass by in the river at the bottom of the garden). They are seen daily at close range from mid-June to mid-December. One group in particular has been habituated and will play around the lodge's boats, almost within touching distance.

The lodge is also one of the best places to see the normally elusive Brazilian tapir. There are wooden viewing platforms just a few minutes' walk from the main buildings, with an excellent sightings record. It has special observation towers, too, for a variety of other wildlife. One is 100 feet high, for observing black howler monkeys; another overlooks a treetop jabiru nest. It is also possible to see black-striped tufted capuchins, black-tailed marmosets and South American coatis along the many trails.

The garden is a great place for wildlife watching and photography, with hummingbirds, tame black-collared hawks, jabiru, chestnut-eared aracaris, several species of kingfisher and a profusion of other birds. There are capybara wandering around the breakfast tables and crab-eating foxes visit at night. Spotlighting, from open cars or small trucks, is a great way of seeing some of the nocturnal wildlife such as ocelots, crab-eating raccoons, southern tamanduas and – very occasionally – jaguars.

Hotel Porto Jofre

At the end of the Transpantaneira Highway, right on the Cuiabá River, this is the best area to see jaguar anywhere in the

WHEN TO GO

The best time to go is during the **dry season**, which usually lasts from **late April to early November** and is when the animals congregate around shrinking areas of open water. July and August are the busiest months. The **rainy season** usually lasts from mid-November to early April (water levels peak around February); this is an interesting, albeit more difficult, time to visit. Much of the wildlife is clustered on scattered islands on higher ground, but dense vegetation can make spotting anything difficult. **Temperatures** can be unbearably high in November, December and January, which is also when **mosquitoes** are out in force.

HOW TO DO IT

Fly to Brasília, São Paulo or Rio de Janeiro and on to Cuiabá, the capital of Mato Grosso and gateway to the northern Pantanal. Then drive about 60 miles south to Poconé, to join the **Transpantaneira Highway**. This 90-mile two-lane dirt road takes you into the heart of the Pantanal. It is raised above the surrounding countryside and, in theory, is open year-round (though a 4WD is essential during the rains). **Be careful when driving** over the bridges, which are in various states of disrepair (many are missing planks). You can hire a vehicle at the airport, or most lodges offer transfers from Cuiabá.

There are a dozen **lodges and hotels** of varying quality along the Transpantaneira, offering accommodation and tours with local guides. There are **boat trips, 4WD and horseback safaris**, and opportunities to **explore on foot** (despite the presence of jaguars and caiman, many areas are considered safe to walk – but beware gangs of white-lipped peccaries). The lodges themselves are often outstanding for wildlife: many of the gardens have more animals than entire reserves in other parts of the world. Since the Transpantaneira passes through a range of **different habitats**, each lodge has its own distinctive wildlife specialities, so stay in several widely separate locations to see the greatest variety of species.

cats' range. Most sightings are within striking distance of the conjunction between the Cuiabá, Three Brothers and Piquiri rivers, which is about an hour away by boat. When I was last at Hotel Porto Jofre, a jaguar suddenly appeared on the riverbank right opposite the hotel.

But it's not just jaguars. Boat trips into jaguar country often encounter giant otter, neotropical otter, Brazilian tapir, ocelot and a host of birds. There is a lagoon behind the hotel, chock-full of giant waterlilies, which is great for ibises, storks, screamers and other species. Hyacinth macaws and toco toucans are resident in the garden, while other locals include fawn-breasted wren and chestnut-bellied guan.

Pantanal Jaguar Camp

Also at Porto Jofre, at the end of the Transpantaneira, is a comfortable but simple (and often noisy) tented camp on a bank of the Cuiabá River.

The wildlife here is similar to that of its nearest neighbour, Hotel Porto Jofre. If you stay for a week (especially from mid-June to October) your chances of seeing a jaguar are very good indeed.

Water wings: The Chatham Islands are home to a mind-boggling variety of birds, including the Buller's albatross

Checking out the
CHATHAMS

New Zealand: Chatham Islands

Despite stiff competition from other seriously offbeat archipelagos, the Chatham Islands have their own very special appeal

The experience ☐

What? Getting close to endemic and endangered birds plus everything from fur seals to great white sharks

Where? A remote archipelago in the South Pacific, 500 miles east of New Zealand

How? Fly from New Zealand, stay in a small hotel and be looked after by a local 'host'

I've been to the Chatham Islands fewer times than anywhere else in this book – just once, in fact, while filming *Last Chance to See*. But it made an indelible impression on me and, by the time the book is published, I will have been back for a second visit.

The Chatham Islands are a tiny archipelago 500 miles east of Christchurch, New Zealand. Barely a dot on the world map, they're home to about 600 hardy souls of mixed European, Maori and Polynesian descent. There are two inhabited islands – Chatham (by far the largest) and Pitt – surrounded by eight smaller islands and countless islets, rocks and stacks, spanning a total radius of about 25 miles.

The Chathams sit slap-bang on the international dateline; indeed, Pitt Island (population: 35) is further east than any other inhabited island in the world. This

My best day

We hitched a ride to South East Island on a crayfishing boat, watching bottlenose dolphins, Buller's and royal albatrosses, sooty shearwaters and red-billed gulls on the way. After landing on a rocky beach, and tiptoeing past several fur seals and two endemic shore plovers, we walked through some thick bushes into a shady woodland. Almost immediately a little bird appeared on a thin branch right in front of me. It was a black robin, once the most critically endangered creature on the planet. I would have travelled to the other side of the world just for that moment – it was the bird I had wanted to see for most of my adult life.

means that Pitt Islanders are the first to see sunrise every day. It also means that a fisherman leaving Pitt today can sail a few miles east and suddenly be in tomorrow. Or is it yesterday? It's all very confusing.

The Chathams are a friendly place, with the quiet charm of a secluded Cornish fishing village. Everyone waves to everyone else and visitors are welcomed with open arms. The landscape is rugged, with an array of volcanic peaks, majestic cliffs, peat bogs, sandy beaches, rocky shores, and trees leaning away from the wind.

The Chatham Islands are renowned for their endemic birds (although there are also many endemic invertebrates, fish and plants). Evolution has been able to design new species without outside interference, so one in every four bird species (and more sub-species) in this little Garden of Eden is found nowhere else. The Chatham oystercatchers on the beach by the hotel, the Chatham Island tui feeding next to the only real tar-sealed road, and the Chatham and Pitt Island shags on the wharf, are all endemic species or sub-species.

Unfortunately, many of them are also endangered. When humans arrived (Polynesians 800-1,000 years ago, then Europeans just over 200 years ago) they brought cats, dogs, rats, possums and a variety of other alien mammals with them, which caused havoc with the local wildlife. A mind-boggling one-third of the 64 species that once bred on the islands are now extinct, including a penguin, a swan, a duck and several flightless rails. Many others plummeted to dangerously low population levels. But conservation programmes are progressively removing alien mammals from key spots, with considerable success.

The Chathams are internationally important breeding grounds for ocean-going seabirds, with a number of species having their main or only world breeding sites on the islands. Some, such as the northern royal albatross, breed in relatively large numbers, but others are on the critical list. The Chatham Island taiko, or Magenta petrel, is one of the world's rarest seabirds: once thought extinct, it breeds only in the Tuku Nature Reserve on Chatham Island. Another species, the

SPECIES CHECKLIST

- Black robin
- Chatham Island warbler, or gerygone
- Forbes' parakeet
- Chatham Island snipe
- Chatham oystercatcher
- Shore plover
- Chatham Island shag
- Pitt Island shag
- Chatham Island taiko, or Magenta petrel
- Chatham petrel
- Chatham albatross, or mollymawk
- Buller's albatross
- Northern royal albatross
- Red-billed gull
- Buff weka
- White-fronted tern
- Chatham Island pigeon
- Chatham Island tui
- Chatham Island tomtit
- Little blue penguin
- Bottlenose dolphin
- New Zealand fur seal
- Great white shark
…and many more

Chatham albatross, is commoner but breeds only in an area of 25 acres on Pyramid Rock.

But the jewel in the Chatham Islands ornithological crown is a rather unremarkable little bird: the black robin. Never happier than when foraging among leaf litter on the forest floor, hunting for cockroaches, wetas and worms, it is the kind of bird you would be forgiven for overlooking. But it does have two claims to fame: the soles of its feet are yellow; and it came closer to extinction (without actually vanishing altogether) than any other animal on the planet. At one point, in 1980,

"At one point, in 1980, there was just a single breeding pair of black robins left – now there are between 200 and 250… and counting"

Beauty and the beak: The shore plover is endemic to the islands

Left: You might spot a Chatham oystercatcher on the beach right by your hotel or seabirds on the cliffs

Need to know

WHEN TO GO

The best months to visit are **late September to March** (during the southern spring and summer). The weather is surprisingly mild at this time of year (though the old adage 'if you don't like the weather, just wait a minute' applies here) and the birds are breeding. **Fur seals** give birth mainly in December; the population peaks in early January. Spring is best for **wild flowers** while the Chatham Island **Forget-Me-Not Festival** is held in October. **Great white shark watching** and cage-diving runs from November to June.

HOW TO DO IT

Access is via New Zealand. There are **scheduled flights from Wellington, Auckland, Christchurch and Napier** (flying time: 1.5-2 hours). There is no regular shipping service, although a freight ship sometimes takes a few passengers (sailing time: 4-5 days from New Zealand).

The **main town is Waitangi**, on Chatham Island, with some 200 residents; this is a good base and home to a number of endemics. Accommodation is limited and must be booked in advance; camping is not illegal, but discouraged outside Waitangi. There is **no scheduled public transport** within the islands – no taxis, even – but it is possible to arrange overland and inter-island transport. **Chartering a fishing boat** is possible, albeit expensive. You can also hire a car: there is one tar-sealed road, between Waitangi and Te One, but the others are mainly gravel.

PACIFIC OCEAN

Te One
Waitangi

Chatham Island

Tuku NR

Pitt Straight

Mangere

Pitt Island

South East Island

Pyramid Rock

0   40km

Most of the archipelago is privately owned and access to many areas is strictly by permission of the owners. There are also a number of environmentally sensitive areas, with **restricted or prohibited access**. However, there are guided tours with permission to visit many such places. Visits to Mangere and South East Islands (homes of the black robin) are by permit only. There is also **a wonderful 'host system'**, whereby a local looks after you, organises tours and calls on other islanders to help you get the most from your stay.

there was just a single breeding pair left – a female called Old Blue and her mate Old Yellow (named for the colour of their leg bands). But thanks to a daring and dramatic rescue operation there are now between 200 and 250... and counting. It's one of the most remarkable conservation success stories of all time.

The only native mammals in the Chatham Islands are marine, with five seal species and 25 whale and dolphin species recorded to date. The New Zealand fur seal is the only pinniped breeding in the archipelago, and the only one that visitors are likely to see. After decades

of commercial whaling, whale populations have been slow to recover. But look out for bottlenose dolphins, long-finned pilot whales, sperm whales and other species while travelling between the islands. The archipelago is actually one of the world's stranding hotspots – among those beaching themselves have been no fewer than eight species of beaked whales.

The Chathams also have a significant population of great white sharks – one estimate suggests up to 200 individuals. They can be seen on boat trips, but there are also opportunities to cage-dive with them.

Polar bears in peril:
Svalbard's bear
population is recovering
after years of hunting –
now global warming is
their biggest threat

Cruising with POLAR BEARS

Arctic Norway: Svalbard

Who wouldn't like to see a wild polar bear? With more bears than people, this remote icy wilderness at the top of the world is the best place to do it

The experience

What? A safari with a difference to watch polar bears, walruses and myriad other high Arctic wildlife

Where? The archipelago of Svalbard, far north-west of mainland Norway and a mere 680-930 miles from the North Pole

How? A comfortable expedition aboard a ship with an ice-strengthened hull

It is possible to see polar bears in many parts of the Arctic and sub-Arctic but apart from tourist-crazy Churchill, in northern Canada, Svalbard is one of the easiest – and wildest – places for a close encounter. There are believed to be 3,000 bears in the archipelago and surrounding frozen seas; if you join an expedition cruise in July, you would be very unlucky not to see quite a few of them.

Svalbard is a dramatic and awe-inspiring wilderness of huge blue and white glaciers, snow-covered mountains and steep-sided fjords. It consists of three main islands – the biggest and better-known Spitsbergen, Nordaustlandet and Edgeøya – as well as many smaller ones.

It is also home to the northernmost permanent settlements on earth. Some 2,700 people live in three main communities: Longyearbyen (the capital

My best day

The final 24 hours of my most recent trip to Svalbard sums it all up. It began with an unforgettable close encounter – a mother polar bear and her two boisterous cubs – and continued with a fin whale, some bearded seals and several species of seabirds around the ship. We spent a thrilling night picking our way through the ice-choked entrance to Isfjorden before disembarking, to the ever-present cacophony of Arctic terns, in the remote capital of Longyearbyen. A short bus ride to the airport gave us a brief glimpse of one of the Arctic foxes that frequently loiter around town, before it was time to check in. But it didn't end there. As we queued to go through security, we spotted nearly 100 beluga whales milling around in the shallow waters right outside the terminal.

and oldest settlement in the archipelago, population 2,000); Ny-Ålesund (permanent population 40, though more during the summer); and a Russian mining town called Barentsburg (population 700). There are no roads between them – people get about by boat in summer and snowmobile in winter – and, apart from a few research and mining outposts, the remainder of Svalbard's 24,000 square miles is almost entirely devoid of human life.

One of the most northerly landmasses in the world – separated from the North Pole by a few hundred miles of frozen ocean (the north coast is about 81°N) – the archipelago is imprisoned by ice for eight months of the year and gripped by perpetual darkness for four. But during the brief Arctic summer it undergoes an extraordinary transformation. This forbidding place turns into a land of 24-hour daylight, with flower-filled tundra, towering sea cliffs crowded with

millions of seabirds, and a crazy-paving of ice that provides a home for polar bears, walruses and ringed and bearded seals.

Polar bears

The primary aim of most trips to Svalbard is to see polar bears. They can be found almost anywhere; in fact, the only place you are guaranteed never to see one is on your ship. But there are certain well-known hotspots and, since they favour areas with plenty of ice, they are less often seen in the west of Spitsbergen. Some individuals spend the summer on land, waiting for the sea to freeze again, but many follow the retreating ice and move into the fjords of the extreme north, north-east and east. They often hunt at glacier fronts, especially in spring when they are looking for ringed seals and their pups.

Polar bear hunting was banned in Svalbard in 1973, after 100 years of intensive exploitation, and the population has recovered significantly in recent

decades. A small number are killed each year in defence of people or property – the number increasing with escalating numbers of visitors to the region. But the greatest concern for the future of polar bears is global warming. They spend much of their lives on sea ice, hunting year-round for ringed seals and, to a lesser extent, bearded seals and sometimes walruses and belugas. But their sea ice habitat is disappearing fast. The winter freeze is coming later and the summer ice is melting earlier and faster. So the bears have to spend more time on land, where it is much harder to find food, and have to swim longer distances between patches of ice, which burns precious fat reserves.

Other wildlife

It's not just polar bears that make Svalbard a top wildlife destination. On land, reindeer can be seen almost anywhere; smaller and shaggier than their mainland relatives, they are particularly common in Reinsdyrflya

SPECIES CHECKLIST

- Polar bear
- Arctic fox
- Reindeer
- Walrus
- Bearded seal
- Ringed seal
- Harp seal
- Fin whale
- Minke whale
- Ivory gull
- Sabine's gull
- Ross's gull
- Glaucous gull
- Arctic tern
- King eider
- Brünnich's guillemot
- Black guillemot
- Little auk
- Puffin
… and many more

"In summer it turns into a place of 24-hour daylight, flowery tundra and a crazy-paving of ice, home to polar bears, walruses and seals"

"The most commonly encountered whales are belugas – herds of anything from a few individuals to a few hundred"

and Nordenskiöldlandet. Arctic foxes are not quite so easy to find, but they frequently patrol underneath seabird colonies, hunting for fallen eggs and chicks, and can be very tame in Longyearbyen, where several people feed them.

Walruses haul out at a number of well-known sites throughout the archipelago, though mostly in the east. They were once abundant in the region, but were hunted almost to extinction for their ivory tusks during three and a half centuries of heavy commercial exploitation. They have been a protected species since 1952 and numbers are slowly beginning to recover: the latest population estimate is about 2,000. Moffen Island – a ring-shaped pebble island – is one of the most important haul-outs; it is strictly protected and no-one is allowed within 300 metres (1,000 feet) of it. Other sites include Poole Pynten, on Prins Karls Forland, and Torrelneset.

The commonest seal in the archipelago is the ringed seal, closely followed by the bearded seal; both can be seen in the water or lying on ice floes. Harp and hooded seals can also be seen around the pack ice, especially in the north-east. Harbour seals breed around Prins Karls Forland, in the west, marking the northernmost limit of their range.

Whale watching in Svalbard must have been exceptionally good 400 years ago, when there were huge populations of several different species. But intensive hunting, from the 17th century until early in the 20th century, virtually wiped them out. They have never really recovered. Traces of the slaughter – from scattered whale bones to blubber ovens – can be found throughout the archipelago. Live baleen whales are harder to find. Bowheads, for example, were once common but are now seen only rarely. Fin and minke whales are encountered on most trips (if there are hard-working and observant naturalists on board) especially off the relatively ice-free western and southern coasts. Humpback whales occur from time to time.

The most commonly encountered whales are belugas – herds of anything from a few individuals to a few hundred. They were hunted when the larger whales became scarce, but seem to be recovering well and are widespread close to shore. Summer hotspots include: Longyearbyen (on the western side of Adventdalen River

mouth, outside the airport and at Sveagruva); elsewhere, the Bellsund-Van Mijenfjorden-Van Keulenfjorden area of the west coast of Spitsbergen is probably the best region. Narwhal sometimes occur in the northern parts of Svalbard, especially around Nordaustlandet and Hinlopenstretet.

Svalbard isn't known for its diversity of birds: although some 160 species have been recorded, only 25 are regular breeders. But what it lacks in variety it more than makes up for in sheer numbers. The starling-sized little auk is the most numerous species in the archipelago, with about one million breeding pairs in no fewer than 207

Gjelder hele Svalbard

Above: Do not ignore the warnings – polar bears are not to be messed with

Right: Keeping a safe distance, watching from the safety of a Zodiac

Below: I am the walrus, showing off some impressive tusks

Need to know

WHEN TO GO

Expedition cruises operate mainly from **early June to August**. This is the high season, when the sun never sets, the pack ice has usually melted sufficiently to allow access to many of the best wildlife sites, and activity at seabird colonies is at its peak. The **midnight sun** stays until around 20 August. Most

young birds have left their nests by the end of the third week in July. If you want to attempt a **circumnavigation cruise** (one that tries to go all the way round Spitsbergen, the main island) go in late July or August.

It is also possible to go in **winter** (many locals say that February is their favourite month!) and base yourself in Longyearbyen or onboard the *Noorderlicht*, a schooner frozen into the ice. A unique experience, with opportunities for **husky-sledding and snowmobiling**, but not generally so good for spotting wildlife.

HOW TO DO IT

Expedition cruises (typically lasting 7-14 days) leave **Longyearbyen** almost daily during the height of summer. **Fly there (via Tromsø or Oslo)** the day before (in case your flight or luggage is delayed) and stay overnight in one of several comfortable hotels or guesthouses before boarding. You can **go there by ship**, too, but only during the summer. Some operators offer tours combining Svalbard with northern Scotland, the Faroe Islands, Iceland, Jan Mayen, Bear Island or Greenland.

You sleep and travel onboard the ship, but go ashore and explore further afield in **inflatable Zodiacs**. Shore landings are in the company of armed guards – always on the lookout for polar bears. Pick your ship wisely; for the best wildlife experience it should have naturalists onboard, and carry **no more than 100 passengers** or so.

Alternatively, it is possible to **stay in Longyearbyen** and arrange excursions lasting from one to several days. Travel is by ski, snowmobile, boat or helicopter and you can go fossil hunting, join flower-walks, go **wildlife-watching by kayak** or join boat trips. However, this isn't necessarily the best way to explore polar bear country – unless you have a gold American Express card and loads of time.

colonies, mostly in western Spitsbergen; in some places, the air is filled with little auks wheeling and turning like mosquitoes over a pond. Brünnich's guillemot comes a close second with some 850,000 breeding pairs in 142 colonies, mainly in south-eastern Spitsbergen. There are also some fabulous gulls (ivory, Ross's, Sabine's and glaucous among them) and, right outside the hotels in Longyearbyen, there are snow buntings, purple sandpipers and grey phalaropes.

Cruise routes

Cruise routes vary from trip to trip, depending on ice and weather conditions, but highlights might include: glaciers, such as Monaco and 14th of July; Magdalenefjord (tucked away in the far north-west but, thanks to its picture-postcard scenery, probably the most photographed landmark in Svalbard); the former whaling station at Smeerenburg; a multitude of terrific wildlife sites; and a community or research base.

Thanks to the Gulf Stream, the west coast has a surprisingly mild climate for its northerly latitude (the average temperature in the height of summer is 42°F/6°C) and is relatively easy to navigate during summer. The wilder, colder, icier north and east are less accessible, but are worth the effort – they tend to have much of the best wildlife.

All a-flutter: For two months of the year, millions of bats roost in a tiny corner of Zambia, dispersing every night to gorge on fruits

Hanging around with
BATS

Zambia: *Kasanka National Park*

When eight million bats get together in Zambia, the result is one of the world's greatest wildlife spectacles – a positively Biblical sight

The experience

What? A twice-daily blizzard of eight million straw-coloured fruit bats

Where? A small clump of trees in a remote corner of central Zambia

How? Stand next to the roost at sunrise and sunset

For a few short weeks every year, unimaginable numbers of straw-coloured fruit bats gather in a clump of trees in Kasanka National Park, close to the border with the Democratic Republic of Congo. They are the second largest bats in Africa – with an average wingspan of more than 30 inches – and they congregate in an area smaller than Buckingham Palace gardens. There are so many of them that branches break under their weight.

Bats are not easy to count, but scientists estimate the size of colony to be between five and 15 million: eight million is the widely accepted figure. With roughly four times as many individuals as in the famous Mara-Serengeti wildebeest migration in Kenya and Tanzania, that makes this the largest aggregation of mammals in Africa.

About 325 miles north-east of Lusaka, Kasanka consists of 150 square miles of

"Stand directly underneath the flightpath and you will be honoured with a sticky shower of faeces, urine and vomit"

My best day

The daily routine is simple: get up at 3.45am, drive in the dark to the roost, and wait. By the time the sun is peeping over the horizon, soon after 5am, the sky has filled with noisily-chattering bats returning from their night-time feast. Settling down for the day, they hang upside-down from every available branch and trunk, literally filling the forest – bats, bats, bats everywhere. The night-time ritual is much the same: you wait on the edge of the forest as the sun sets and, soon after 6pm, all eight million bats rise from the trees and fly out into the darkness. It is mind-boggling – quite simply, every day is a best day.

elevated plain covered in miombo woodland and dotted with plains, lakes, rivers and swamps. It was Zambia's first privately-managed national park. It's not a traditional safari destination – don't expect large herds of animals around every corner – but it does have several claims to fame.

In particular, it is home to the world's densest population of sitatunga. Anyone who has spent hours in mosquito-infested swamps searching fruitlessly for this elusive amphibious antelope will appreciate Kasanka: from Fibwe Tree Hide (reputed to be the best sitatunga viewing place in Africa) seeing 20 before breakfast is by no means unusual. No fewer than 110 mammal species have been recorded in the park: you are likely to see the rare blue monkey, elephant, hippo, side-striped jackal and yellow baboon, as well as considerable numbers of puku antelope.

Birdlife is especially prolific. With a bird list exceeding 450 species so far, Kasanka

offers some of the finest bird-watching in Africa. Raptors are everywhere and it's a great place to see everything from big, brightly-coloured Ross's turacos to Pel's fishing owls. There are also shoebills at Bangweulu Swamps, just up the road.

There are lots of creepy-crawlies, too. I've encountered more wildlife in the thatch-roofed chalets at Wasa Camp, in the heart of the park, than I have in entire national parks elsewhere. Expect to come across black-and-orange-striped tiger snakes, wonderfully hairy baboon spiders, green praying mantises and a menagerie of moths, cockroaches, millipedes and ants (huge biting ants are everywhere).

But all that pales into insignificance compared with one of the greatest wildlife spectacles on earth. The twice-daily blizzard of flying foxes is more than ample compensation for a few nips and bites.

The bats are believed to migrate from all over Central Africa, descending on a 30-acre area of mushitu swamp forest near the confluence of the Musola and Kasanka rivers. Appearing like clockwork each year, they come to feed on the seasonal fruits which weigh down the trees for miles around. Many of the bats are pregnant females, or females carrying newborn pups, and they need all that extra energy – they arrive just before the peak of fruit production and leave as the availability of fruit declines. The colony is believed to eat some 5,000 tonnes of wild loquat, red milkwood and other fruit every night.

SPECIES CHECKLIST

- Straw-coloured fruit bat
- African elephant
- Sitatunga
- Puku
- Black lechwe
- Sable antelope
- Roan antelope
- Common duiker
- Lichtenstein's hartebeest
- Buffalo
- Hippopotamus
- Leopard
- Side-striped jackal
- African civet
- Angolan genet
- Cape clawless otter
- Marsh mongoose
- Thick-tailed bushbaby
- Yellow baboon
- Blue monkey
- Vervet monkey
- Pel's fishing owl
- Crowned eagle
- African fish eagle
- African marsh harrier
- White-backed vulture
- Hooded vulture
- Saddle-billed stork
- Nile crocodile
… and many more

The bats spend all day hanging upside-down in tightly-packed clusters on every available branch and tree trunk. They are great fun to watch – restless, always chattering, fidgeting and shuffling from one position to another. Occasionally, one squeezes out of the throng, clambers over all the other bats and hangs from the lowest individual to get in position for a pee – without drenching its bedfellows – before shaking itself dry and clambering back.

Just hanging: The bats spend their days dangling in clusters

Left: Hides provide up-close viewing, while you can get the wider picture on a game drive

Need to know

WHEN TO GO

The first bats have ususally arrived by **20 October** and usually stay at least until **Christmas** (the whole colony has gone within a week of the first individuals departing). The rainy season lasts from November to April: typically, there are occasional showers in November and daily showers in December. It's a pleasant relief after months of heat and dust – and Kasanka is at its most beautiful during the rains, with green grass, flowers everywhere and bright clear skies. Bird-watching is especially good in the rainy season, too, when migrants swell the bird list. The park is open year-round.

HOW TO DO IT

Hire a car and drive from Lusaka. It takes six or seven hours and the roads are tarred and in pretty good condition as far as the park entrance. Beware heavy rains and occasional police roadblocks targeting tourists for money.

Alternatively, park authorities will organise a **small plane** to fly you from anywhere in Zambia to a small airstrip within the protected area. Flying takes about 1.5 hours from Lusaka and, split between several people, does not cost much more than driving.

Stay at **Wasa Lodge**, a collection of rondavels (African-style huts) and simple chalets, a short drive from the bat roost. There is also a basic campsite near the roost (you will need your own tents, equipment and food).

At the bat roost, you can either wait outside the forest or watch from one of several wooden hides. The best is **Fibwe Tree Hide**, 60 feet up a giant mahogany tree – you need to be fairly agile (and have a good head for heights) to get up the narrow wooden ladder to the top, but the panoramic views over Fibwe Swamp and the roost are spectacular.

In between bat flights, there is a choice of escorted game drives, walking, bicycle and canoe safaris. There are relatively few dangerous animals in the park (although lions and hyenas can wander through). **Bangweulu Swamps**, some 30 miles north, is also worth a visit: it is home to over 100,000 black lechwe and is your best chance to see shoebills.

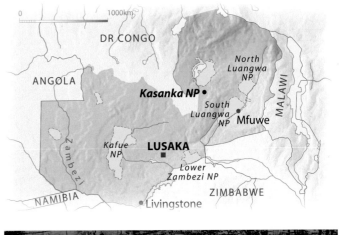

Unsurprisingly, the roost attracts lots of predators and scavengers – many loitering on the forest floor, ready to snatch any bats unlucky enough to fall. Eagles, vultures, black mambas, water monitors, crocodiles, civets and leopards are among them.

My favourite time at Kasanka is first thing in the morning, waiting for the bats to return. You hear them before you see them: a distinctive squeakity-squeak as they begin to pour in from the countryside.

First, there are little groups of 10, or 20. Then there are hundreds. Then thousands. Soon the sky is bursting with millions of giant bats. And for the next hour it simply doesn't stop. Stand directly underneath the flightpath and you will be honoured with a sticky shower of faeces, urine and vomit. Then the sun is shining, the bats have dropped into the forest, and you have to wait until evening, to watch them take-off once again for their next nightly foray.

Here be monsters: The Komodo dragon – 200lbs and 10 feet of bacteria-drooling malevolence

Running from KOMODO DRAGONS

Indonesia: Komodo Island

How can you like a place that is home to a giant, man-eating lizard that lunges at you with a spine-tingling hiss? I have no idea – but I do

The experience

What? Braving a small slice of heaven (or hell, depending on your point of view), where you can see legendary Komodo dragons

Where? Komodo National Park, in the Lesser Sunda Islands, 300 miles east of Bali

How? Travel there by boat, then hike around

I'm not sure what it is about Komodo. I didn't enjoy my first visit at all. It seemed quite a desolate and unwelcoming place, and I had a sense of unease the whole time I was there (initially sparked by the deer that were hanging around on the beach, near the landing site, too nervous to venture into the interior).

To make matters worse, it was unbearably hot, I had more dangerously close encounters with venomous snakes during a single week there than in all my previous travels put together and – to be honest – I found the famous Komodo dragons to be animals of minimal appeal.

But that was over 20 years ago and, since then, I've actually grown to love this little corner of Indonesia. Like the venom from a snake bite, somehow it gets into the blood and stays there. I'm not pretending it's as lovely as most of my other favourite places

– and maybe it's an acquired taste – but there is indisputably nowhere else quite like it. Give it a chance and you will realise that it is very special in its own peculiar way. Even the Komodo dragon itself – over 200lbs and 10 feet of malevolence, wrapped in loose, leathery skin, and with a mouth that drips with fetid, bacteria-filled saliva – has its own particular charm.

Indonesia has about 18,000 islands altogether (no one can agree on the exact number) and Komodo dragons live on just five of them, close to the centre of the archipelago. These are Komodo itself, the neighbouring island of Rinca (sometimes spelled 'Rintja'), the islets of Gili Motang and Gili Dasami, and a very tiny corner of Flores. Together, they provide a home for about 1,400 dragons (previous estimates of nearer 5,000 are believed to have been a miscalculation). Unfortunately, only about 50 of them are breeding females, so the great concern is that, because they have such a limited range, a forest fire, a disease outbreak or a sudden decline in prey species could wipe out the entire breeding population in one fell swoop.

Lying about 300 miles east of Bali (the two islands are so dissimilar that they might as well be on different planets), Komodo itself is quite a small island measuring just 22 miles by nine miles. Rather appropriately, its hills undulate like the great heavy folds of a lizard's skin and its peaks are jagged and fang-like. The highest point is Gunung Satalibo, at 2,411 feet: despite the unbearable heat, the rather strenuous hike to the top is worth it for the breathtaking views. During the dry season, Komodo looks altogether quite sinister – scorched, dry and dusty. But during the rainy season much of it is luxuriantly green and it looks remarkably Welsh or Scottish.

There are certainly no other similarities with Wales or Scotland – not least in terms of the local inhabitants. There is an old joke that the animals on Komodo can be divided into three main categories: highly venomous, mildly venomous, and large, scary and drooling. It is believed to have more venomous snakes per square foot than anywhere else on the planet: Indian spitting cobras, Russell's pit vipers, white-lipped vipers and green tree vipers among them. It is certainly one of those places where you have to check for fatal surprises at every turn, whether it's inside your boots, behind a bush or underneath a toilet seat. Even one of its geckos is more reminiscent of a surly bulldog than a wide-eyed lizard.

But it's the Komodo dragon that is undisputed king. For centuries, the Chinese returned from Komodo (where they were looking for its underwater treasure trove of pearls) with stories of great scaly man-eating monsters with fiery breath – stories that are believed to have been the origin of the Chinese dragon myth, or at least to have enhanced it. The Komodo dragon is, after all, a large creature with scales, it is a man-eater, and though it doesn't actually

Violent yet vulnerable:
There are thought to be
around 1,500 Komodo
dragons, but only 50
breeding females

SPECIES CHECKLIST

- Komodo dragon
- Timor deer
- Water buffalo
- Wild boar
- Crab-eating macaque
- Palm civet
- Komodo rat
- Dugong
- Lombok flying fox
- Green imperial pigeon
- Greater crested tern
- Gull-billed tern
- Red-tailed tropicbird
- Orange-footed megapode
- Lesser sulphur-crested cockatoo
- Beach stone curlew
- Brahminy kite
- Osprey
- White-bellied sea eagle
- Short-toed eagle
- Bonelli's eagle
- Variable goshawk
- Brown goshawk
- Australian hobby
- Spotted kestrel
- Savanna nightjar
- Blue-tailed bee-eater
- Green turtle
- Hawksbill turtle
- Indian cobra
- Russell's pit viper
- Green tree viper
- White-lipped viper
- Tokay gecko
- Komodo bow-fingered gecko

...and many more

"You wouldn't want to get bitten by a Komodo dragon – they dribble all the time, their saliva a witch's brew of 57 varieties of toxic bacteria"

breathe fire, it is reputed to have the worst breath of any creature known to man. People at the time used to write 'Here be dragons' on their maps when they saw a land they didn't like the look of – and Komodo was definitely such a land. It was a place that travellers were warned about for being particularly dangerous and inhospitable.

The rumours persisted, with traders and fishermen bringing back stories of giant prehistoric lizards, but (understandably) no one seriously thought such things existed, except in people's wildest imaginations. Finally, the Dutch sent a scientific expedition to settle the matter. In the spirit of scientific expeditions at the time, they shot a Komodo dragon and sent it back for evaluation. It was identified as a member of the monitor lizard family and nothing short of the largest lizard in the world.

A number of villagers and park rangers boast impressive Komodo dragon scars, so there is no denying that they are dangerous

animals to have living on your doorstep. Over the years, they have even killed one or two tourists. The thing is, if a Komodo dragon wanted to, it could easily take you down with a single, half-hearted swipe of its tail (which is powerful enough to knock an adult water buffalo off its feet). But being able to kill people doesn't necessarily mean that that's what it does. Despite their fearsome reputation, Komodo dragons attack people surprisingly rarely. It's just that wandering around their island home on your own makes you feel a little like a duck walking into a Chinese restaurant.

You certainly wouldn't want to get bitten by a Komodo dragon. They really do dribble all the time and the saliva that pours out of the sides of their mouths is very unpleasant indeed. It contains a witch's brew of no fewer than 57 varieties of toxic bacteria. These are so virulent that, without emergency treatment, a dragon's bite doesn't heal and you have a good chance of dying of septicaemia or some-such disease.

As if that is not enough, recent research suggests that the dragons may also be venomous. Glands in their mouths produce venom as potent as that found in some of the world's most dangerous snakes, making them by far the largest venomous creatures on the planet.

You could almost forgive them all of that, if they were brave and worthy kings of their domain. But far from it: their method of hunting is both sneaky and cruel. When

a Komodo dragon lies in wait for a large animal such as a horse or a water buffalo, it doesn't necessarily expect to kill it there and then. If it gets involved in a fight it might be injured, and there's no benefit in that, so often it will just bite its prey and run away. That awful concoction of saliva and venom ensures the hapless animal will weaken and die, usually within a few days, whereupon the dragon can eat it at leisure (or another dragon can eat it at leisure, if it happens to find it first).

So this is the animal you travel all the way to Komodo to see.

Meet the relatives:
Not a Komodo dragon,
but a water monitor

Opposite: Not merely
dribbling – positively
drooling; Komodo
looking surprisingly
Welsh or Scottish

My best day

My closest encounter with a Komodo dragon came while filming the TV series *Last Chance to See*. We were with a Komodo dragon researcher, Deni, who had set a huge trap under a tree, and had caught a large male. Deni taped its mouth shut (goodness knows how) and four of us tried to hold it still as it struggled with awesome surges of power that nearly sent us flying. We took a few measurements (it was 8.5 feet long) and attached a radio transmitter to its back (like a miniature rucksack) before Deni took off the tape and counted: 'One, two… three!' We all let go and ran so fast it didn't even take measurable time.

The good news is that your chances of success are very good indeed. Initially, it's not so easy because Komodo dragons often lie completely motionless on the ground: you have to keep your eyes peeled, and wits about you, for fear of tripping over them. Once you spot them, they look surprisingly docile; it's ridiculously tempting to edge closer and closer, until you're almost within touching distance. The only proof that they are still alive is an occasional flick of the tongue, which will send you catapulting backwards and remind you not to push your luck so much next time.

But once your eyes are attuned to Komodo dragon spotting, you will see them all over the place. They frequently hang around the ranger stations, looking for scraps, and you can bump into them almost anywhere. The best times to look are early in the morning and late in the afternoon, when they tend to be most active (they doze when the sun is high). A visit during the courting season (May to August) can be particularly exciting – you might see the males standing on their hind legs and wrestling one another in one of their dramatic shows of dominance.

Eventually, you will be hooked. I know this isn't the case, but try to imagine Komodo dragons as the last of all the dinosaurs, left stranded in a small pocket of islands in South-East Asia, and you'll see them in a whole new light. They really are weird and wonderful animals.

There is other wildlife on Komodo, of course, although it does inevitably tend to be overshadowed by the giant in its midst. Komodo sits in a transition zone between Australasian and Asian flora and fauna: many of the mammals are Asiatic in origin, while many of the birds and reptiles are

"The tokay gecko, the second-largest species, has a reputation for being the bulldog of the gecko world – when it bites it won't let go"

Australian. The diversity isn't great, but there are some interesting species here.

Best of all, Komodo is a herpetologist's dream-come-true and there are some outstanding reptiles. Geckos are particularly noticeable, especially if you stay on the island overnight. They include the common house gecko, flat-tailed house gecko, mourning gecko, common four-clawed gecko, Indopacific tree gecko, Darmandville bow-fingered gecko, Komodo bow-fingered gecko and, top of the list – another giant – the tokay gecko. The second-largest gecko in the world, this breathtakingly impressive animal measures up to 15 inches long and makes a shockingly loud call (sounding like 'tokay' or 'gekk-gekk'). It has huge eyes and is almost blue in colour, with impressive

Below: Wild boar, like all other large mammals in the area, appear on the Komodo dragon's menu

bright red or yellow spots. But most of all it has a reputation for being the bulldog of the gecko world, because when it bites it won't let go. (If you're unfortunate enough to get bitten, stroll down to the beach and hold it underwater.) It is commonly found in houses in rural areas and roams the walls and ceilings of the spartan tourist accommodation at night.

Other lizards on Komodo include flying dragons – which use great folds of skin stretched across movable ribs to form 'wings' that enable them to glide as far as 25 feet from tree to tree – and several species of skink.

Snakes are much in evidence – unlike in most parts of the world, where you are lucky to get a fleeting glimpse. Residents include the Indonesian ratsnake, painted bronzeback, common mock viper, Island pipe snake, Indian wolf snake, dog-toothed cat snake, Indian cobra, Russell's pit viper, green tree viper and white-lipped viper. There are more in the sea – the dog-faced water snake and little wart snake among them. Saltwater crocodiles were seen around Komodo in the past, but they have probably disappeared from this part of their range, or occur very rarely.

Mammals on Komodo include Timor deer, water buffalo and wild boar (all introduced by people), as well as palm civets and lots of Lombok flying foxes. There are also wild horses and crab-eating macaques on neighbouring Rinca. The Komodo rat occurs on Rinca and several

neighbouring islands and islets, but has yet to be recorded on Komodo itself.

Among the birds, one of the most interesting is the orange-footed megapode or scrubfowl, which is about the size of a domestic chicken and builds a huge mound of leaf litter and other debris in which to lay its eggs (heat generated by the decomposing organic matter does the job of incubation). The biggest mounds can be 15 feet high and 30 feet across.

The seas around Komodo are still quite rich, despite destructive fishing practices in the area (including blast fishing, cyanide

Herpetologist heaven: The white-lipped tree viper is just one of Komodo's readily spotted snake species

Need to know

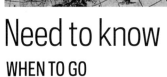

WHEN TO GO

Komodo and Rinca can be **visited year-round**, but two periods are best avoided: the peak of the **monsoon** rains (January-March, though rains can stretch November-April); and the busiest months of July and August. The dry season (**May to October**) is a good time to visit, despite the scorchingly high temperatures. Immediately after the rains is particularly nice, when everything is lush green. There is more Komodo dragon activity from May to August, when they mate, and when the hatchlings emerge from their eggs (April onwards).

HOW TO DO IT

The only way to get to Komodo is by **boat**, either from Labuan Bajo (on the west coast of Flores) or Bima (eastern Sumbawa). Both towns can be reached by scheduled flights from Bali, or by ferry. **Day-trips** are possible to Rinca (two hours from Labuan Bajo) but Komodo is too far. On Komodo there is limited and spartan accommodation at Loh Liang ranger station; there is no accommodation in Kampung Komodo, the only village on the island.

Alternatively, join a **live-aboard boat** for a cruise (departing Bali, Lombok, Bima and Labuan Bajo). Some cruises focus on Komodo; others include it as part of a multi-stop itinerary. Or get a group together and **charter your own boat** (not as difficult as it sounds).

It is inadvisable to **hike** without a local guide or ranger, who knows where to find dragons and keeps you safe. Short walks leave from Loh Liang to the Banugulung viewing area (two hours round-trip). **Longer walks**, lasting one or two days, are also possible, staying the night in a spartan ranger post at Loh Sebita or Loh Genggo.

The neighbouring island of **Rinca** has its own Komodo dragons. There is limited and spartan accommodation at Loh Buaya ranger station (which also offers guided walks). Hiking on Rinca has the added attraction of seeing wild horses and **crab-eating macaques** (which are not present on Komodo).

fishing and the collection of live fish for the tropical fish trade). With a variety of coral reefs, seagrass beds and mangrove forests there is a lot to see. There are often strong currents and visibility close to shore varies from quite good to terrible, so take advice before snorkelling or diving. Depending on the dive site, there is a good variety of hard and soft corals, colourful sea urchins, Spanish dancers, several species of sea turtle (mainly green and hawksbill) and plenty of fish life.

Manta rays occur in large numbers, feeding on plankton blooms (mainly from September to January). There are also frogfish, Napoleon wrasse, big potato cod, dogfish tuna and some huge groupers.

Although sharks aren't as numerous as they once were, there is a good chance of seeing grey reef and white-tipped reef sharks, while hammerheads and bronze whalers often aggregate around Langkoi Rock from July to September. Whale sharks also occur from time to time. Dugongs are known to live in the area (though they are not seen very often) and more than a dozen different whales and dolphins have been recorded.

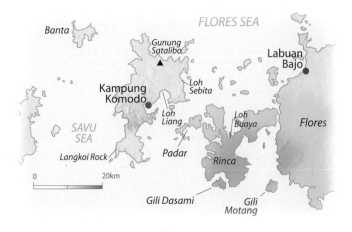

Big softie: Although generously proportioned, manatees are graceful and hugely inquistive

Being hugged by
MANATEES

Florida: Crystal River National Wildlife Refuge

All you need for this wildlife encounter with a difference is an ability to snorkel and a penchant for big, friendly animals that want to hug you

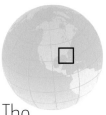

The experience

What? Snorkelling with West Indian manatees in clear, warm, shallow water

Where? Just two hour's drive from Orlando

How? Stay in a hotel and take a half-day boat trip (drive yourself or join a guided tour)

What looks like a tuskless walrus (with flabby jowls, bristly whiskers and thick leathery skin), behaves like an underwater cow and is Florida's official state marine mammal? It's the Florida manatee – a sub-species of the West Indian manatee.

Florida manatees have a huge summer range that extends from Louisiana, along both coasts of Florida and up as far as Virginia. But the best time to see them is in winter, when falling temperatures drive them to a more restricted range in warmer waters along parts of the Florida coast.

Manatees don't like the cold. Although they're warm-blooded they lose body heat easily and, during sudden freezes, can die surprisingly quickly. So during cold weather they gather in the warm waters of natural springs – in particular, Crystal River, Homosassa Springs, Blue Spring

"While manatees aren't necessarily the most beautiful animals in the world, they are certainly among the most friendly"

My best day

Every day spent snorkelling with manatees is a good day. But I'll never forget finding my perfect manatee house. Hidden away on a bend of the Homosassa River, on Florida's Gulf Coast, it has water on three sides, a swimming pool, and a beautiful wooden sun deck. But, best of all, it has manatees at the bottom of the garden. Sadly, it wasn't for sale – its owners love the manatees too much to contemplate moving. They are retired and can observe them from every room in the house. I often think of them having breakfast in bed, or morning coffee, while watching the manatees swim past the window.

and Warm Mineral Spring – as well as the warm water effluents from at least 10 power plants. Several thousand manatees descend on these hotspots every winter: aerial surveys have counted as few as 1,758 in 2002 but as many as 5,076 in 2010.

They can be seen almost anywhere, including busy marinas and waterways through housing estates, but Crystal River National Wildlife Refuge, on the Gulf of Mexico, is widely regarded as the best site. It is only about 46 acres in size but is home to the largest concentration of these gentle giants in North America (as many as 300 at one time). The water is often sparklingly clear, there are no currents and the water is often no more than waist deep.

The refuge is in King's Bay, which forms the headwaters of the Crystal River. Six hundred million gallons of freshwater flow into the bay every day, from 30-odd natural springs. It flows at a constant temperature of 72°F (22°C), which is

Meet & greet: A volunteer warden in Crystal River with one of his charges

perfect for manatees. They spend nights and mornings crowding around these outflows, and then around noon wander off in search of tasty aquatic plants to eat.

While manatees aren't necessarily the most beautiful animals in the world, they are certainly among the most friendly. They are also very curious – snorkellers simply have to lie on the surface of the water and, soon enough, a manatee will come to investigate. In a single morning, you are likely to see at least ten and perhaps more than 50, including mothers with newborn calves. I've counted over 100 different manatees in less than an hour.

The best sites can get quite crowded, so there are 'Manatee Sanctuary Areas' where manatees can go, but snorkellers cannot. Even the friendliest manatees need a break from time to time. The sanctuaries also provide a safe haven from boats: you'll notice many manatees with scars on their bodies caused by collisions with an ever-increasing number of pleasure craft. There are volunteer wardens in kayaks and rangers from the US Fish and Wildlife Service to keep an official eye on things, but it's hard for them to monitor all the no-go areas and speed restrictions.

The best strategy is to find a quiet corner, and wait for a manatee to find you. I remember once hearing high-pitched squeaking and chirping noises underwater and turning around to see a particularly inquisitive individual coming straight towards me. Although they are rotund and

SPECIES CHECKLIST

- West Indian manatee
- Bottlenose dolphin
- Raccoon
- Bald eagle
- Osprey
- Northern harrier
- Sharp-shinned hawk
- Red-shouldered hawk
- Eastern screech owl
- Barred owl
- Anhinga
- Double-crested cormorant
- Royal tern
- Ring-billed gull
- Laughing gull
- Bonaparte's gull
- Great blue heron
- Black-crowned night heron
- Little blue heron
- Tricoloured heron
- Green heron
- Great egret
- Snowy egret
- White ibis
- Wood stork
- Belted kingfisher
- American white pelican
- Tarpon
- … and many more

rather ponderous animals, manatees are amazingly graceful underwater. We stared at one another for several minutes, looking intently into each other's eyes, as we floated quietly at the surface. When I started to fiddle with my camera, it seemed genuinely interested in what I was doing. It posed beautifully for a few shots, but then took a breath at the surface, sank down to the bottom – and promptly fell asleep. Manatees do that quite often. They just

It takes two... Manatees enjoy rubbing and bumping each other – and will happily get tactile with snorkellers

stop whatever they are doing and have an instant nap. The first time I saw it happen, I thought the animal had died.

Manatees have a flatulence problem, too. They have to eat huge quantities of vegetation and, since they are hindgut fermenters, produce copious amounts of methane gas. Thus they fart more than most animals. The tell-tale bubbles, however, are an excellent way of locating submerged manatees from the surface.

They enjoy body contact, often rubbing and bumping one another, and seem to assume that snorkellers enjoy the same kind of rumbustious exchange. Once, I was photographing one manatee when another suddenly swam up to me and gave me a big manatee hug. It literally held me with its two flippers, as if we were about to launch into an underwater foxtrot. It was quite an experience – considering the animal was 10 feet long and weighed half a tonne.

Need to know

WHEN TO GO

The best time to snorkel with manatees is from **mid-December to the end of March**, when they are concentrated around warm underwater springs. The weather is usually pleasant and sunny at this time of year, with daytime temperatures peaking at around 70-74°F /21-23°C, although early mornings and evenings tend to be cool. Water temperature at the manatee encounter sites average 65-72°F/18-22°C.

Smaller numbers are present year-round, but are harder to find in **summer**. Try to avoid busy weekends and holidays as encounter sites can get crowded. **Mornings are best** – the manatees tend to disperse to feed in the afternoons.

HOW TO DO IT

The 'city' of **Crystal River** (pop. 3,539), a short drive from Tampa and Orlando on Florida's Gulf Coast, is the self-proclaimed 'Home of the Manatee'. Some hotels and guesthouses have manatees at the bottom of the garden, and many companies offer snorkelling tours.

Alternatively, hire your own **small boat** and do it yourself. Top spots within **Crystal River National Wildlife Refuge** include Three Sisters Spring and King's Spring. Homosassa Springs, about 10 miles down the road, is also very good and usually less crowded – though access can be more difficult. All encounters with manatees are conducted under strict federal guidelines to ensure as little disturbance as possible.

In the afternoons, when the manatees are harder to find, join a bird-watching tour (or hire a boat, kayak or canoe) to explore **King's Bay**: there are ospreys, a few bald eagles, and lots of egrets, herons, ibises and pelicans. Bottlenose dolphins frequently turn up, while raccoons are a familiar sight on the water's edge.

Take a trip to nearby **Rainbow River** for an unforgettable two-hour drift snorkel. You get dropped off upstream, and drift along in the current, accompanied by everything from alligator gar (a primitive fish) and freshwater turtles to double-crested cormorants catching fish underwater.

Soaring with
SEA BIRDS

Iceland

I've been to Iceland more than 70 times – and with all its wildlife, breathtaking scenery, ever-changing light and endless space, it's magical every time

The experience

What? Unimaginable numbers of birds (plus whales and other wildlife) in the land of ice and fire

Where? Various hotspots across Iceland, a wild isle in the North Atlantic and the least densely populated country in Europe

How? Join a guided tour or drive yourself

When you come in to land at Keflavík International Airport, and stare out of the window at the dark lava fields, rugged mountain slopes and imposing volcanoes stretched out below, it is hard not to imagine that you are landing on the moon.

The whole landscape speaks aloud of the elemental forces that move continents and build mountains. Iceland is perched on top of the Mid-Atlantic Ridge, which runs right across the country from the south-west to the north-east and marks the exact point at which the Eurasian and American plates are being pulled apart. This 'tear' is the site of intense volcanic and geothermal activity, making Iceland one of the most geologically active places on earth.

It is also one of the most sparsely populated countries. With a population

Puffin parade: The emblem of Iceland, puffins are abundant here – up to ten million in late summer

My best day

I've had so many memorable days in Iceland, but one particular hour stands out. It was just before midnight and I was on a boat in Skjálfandi Bay, just below the Arctic Circle. The sea was glassy calm, the sun was touching the horizon and the entire landscape was bathed in a golden light that I've only ever seen in the far north during midsummer. There were hundreds, if not thousands, of Arctic terns around the boat and the sea was thick with puffins. We had been watching two blue whales in the distance when, at precisely 12 o'clock, a minke whale surfaced right in the glow of the midnight sun.

of only 320,000 – nearly two-thirds of whom live in and around the capital of Reykjavík – most of Iceland's 39,756 square miles is completely devoid of people.

But it would be unfair to describe this absolutely extraordinary country as barren. It is certainly wild, but the stark lunar landscape – once used as a training ground for American astronauts – is only one part of a rich and varied wilderness quite unlike anywhere else on the planet. Dotted with spectacular ice-caps and vast glaciers, bubbling mud pools, hot springs, steaming lava fields, active (and sometimes troublesome) volcanoes, snow-capped peaks, thundering waterfalls and erupting geysers, it is a geologist's paradise.

It is also incredibly rich in wildlife. The biggest attractions are whales (several species), seabirds and a range of colourful wild flowers. But grey and common seals, Arctic foxes, reindeer (imported from Norway) and a variety of other species add to the appeal.

Birds, birds, birds

Nearly 400 bird species have been recorded in Iceland, although many of these have been recorded only once and others no more than a handful of times. Only 77 species are considered regular breeders.

So why is Iceland such a popular destination for bird watchers? First, it has some major 'ticks', including the gyrfalcon, Barrow's goldeneye and harlequin duck. Second, many of the breeding birds are astonishingly abundant. Iceland's vast seabird colonies, especially those at Látrabjarg, Hornbjarg, Hælavíkurbjarg and the Westman Islands, are some of the most impressive in the world.

The best-known species is the Atlantic puffin, the emblem of Iceland, and there is no better place to watch this comical bird. With an estimated population of around three million breeding pairs (total numbers exceed an astronomical ten million birds in late summer), it is hard to miss. Try visiting

the town of Heimaey, in the Westman Islands, in the latter part of August, to watch the local children on Puffin Patrol. They roam the streets saving baby puffins, or 'pufflings', that have left their nests and crash-landed in town. The child who sets the most free becomes 'Puffin Fledgling King' for a year.

Other species breeding in exceptionally large numbers include common and Brünnich's guillemots, razorbills, northern fulmars, black-legged kittiwakes, northern gannets, great skuas and Arctic terns. Iceland is also home to Europe's largest Leach's storm petrel colony, the majority of the world's pink-footed geese, and a third of the European population of eider.

Whales & dolphins

Since the first commercial whale-watching trip left the little south-eastern town of Höfn in 1992, Iceland has grown to become a mecca for whale watchers from all over the world. There are now a number of

SPECIES CHECKLIST

- Puffin
- Brünnich's guillemot
- Common guillemot
- Black guillemot
- Razorbill
- Arctic tern
- Northern gannet
- Gyrfalcon
- White-tailed eagle
- Harlequin duck
- Barrow's goldeneye
- Blue whale
- Humpback whale
- Minke whale
- Orca
- White-beaked dolphin
- Harbour porpoise
- … and many more

Avian smorgasbord: Iceland has some major 'ticks' for bird watchers, including the strikingly beautiful harlequin duck

Left: Grímsey Island is the northernmost part of Iceland; Arctic terns and herring gulls are just two of the local birds

"It has been estimated that more than one million birds (some say two million) nest on Látrabjarg – Iceland's greatest bird cliff"

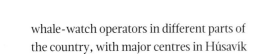

whale-watch operators in different parts of the country, with major centres in Húsavík and Reykjavík. How many capital cities around the world can virtually guarantee whale sightings?

The sheer variety of species being seen is quite remarkable. Minke whales are encountered on almost all trips, while humpback whales, orcas, white-beaked dolphins and harbour porpoises are seen regularly. Iceland is also the only place in Europe – and one of only a handful of locations anywhere in the world – where it is relatively easy to find blue whales.

But it is the spectacular setting, as much as anything else, that draws whale watchers to Iceland. Where else can you encounter minke whales in the orange glow of the midnight sun, watch orcas against a striking backdrop of snow-capped mountains and sail alongside blue whales within sight of the Arctic Circle?

But Iceland is killing whales...

The natural reaction to the awful news that Iceland hunts whales is to avoid the country altogether. But a tourism boycott would damage its burgeoning whale-watch industry, which offers the best solution to the whaling issue in the long-term by making whales worth more alive than dead. What you should do is to boycott any restaurant serving whale meat – so many tourists are trying whale meat 'just once' that they are gobbling up no less than 40% of the market.

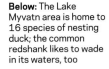

Below: The Lake Myvatn area is home to 16 species of nesting duck; the common redshank likes to wade in its waters, too

WHERE TO GO

There are many wildlife hotspots in Iceland. Here are a few of my favourites:

Eldey Island

Lying just over nine miles off the extreme south-west coast, Eldey's precipitous cliffs rise to a height of 250 feet. This tiny stack is home to one of the largest gannet colonies in the world – 16,000 pairs. This is also where the world's last two surviving great auks once lived. It is illegal to land on Eldey, but it is sometimes possible to arrange a boat trip from the Reykjanes peninsula. Over the years, I have encountered blue, sei, minke, humpback and orca within a stone's throw of the rock.

Lake Mývatn

Located in the north-east, Lake Mývatn is dotted with green islets and set in a spectacular lunar landscape. The vegetation here is luxuriant by Icelandic standards. The lake is not large (it takes about an hour to drive all the way round) but it requires days to explore properly.

It has 16 species of nesting duck – more than anywhere else in Europe – and is home to red-letter species such as gyrfalcons, harlequin ducks, Barrow's goldeneye, incredibly tame red-necked phalaropes and many more. But be warned: 'Mývatn' means 'Midge Lake' – at certain times during summer, the midges gather in dense swarms that, from a distance, look like tall columns of black smoke.

Westman Islands

An archipelago of 15 volcanic islands, just off Iceland's south coast, the Westman Islands are home to more puffins than anywhere else in the world. They also have vast numbers of other seabirds, including Iceland's only breeding colony of manx shearwaters; large numbers of them gather just offshore in the evenings in early summer. The islands are particularly good for orca too.

Látrabjarg

Iceland's greatest bird cliff – the largest in the North Atlantic – is about nine miles long and some 1,500 feet at its highest point. It has been estimated that more than

All at sea: Northern gannets gather on the cliffs of the Langanes peninsula

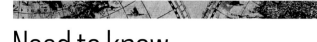

Need to know

WHEN TO GO

The best time is **late May to late August**, when there are long hours of daylight and more fine weather. The nesting season begins in early May, peaks in June and peters out in July. Go mid-June to August for the **best flowers**; don't travel before mid-July if you want to be sure of getting into the uninhabited interior. Most cetaceans are present throughout summer, but **blue whales** are most likely in June and early July. Otherwise, there is something of interest year-round: one tour operator runs a winter adventure offering **orcas and the northern lights** combined.

HOW TO DO IT

There is a wide choice of **guided tours** focusing on the natural history of Iceland. Most concentrate on the coastal areas, with short detours inland, but some drive through the central highlands in specially-converted 4WD high-clearance buses or 'superjeeps'.

To do it yourself, **fly to Keflavík** (the international airport, a 45-minute drive from Reykjavík) and hire a car (or take your own car on a ferry). **Driving in Iceland** is easy and, outside Reykjavík, there is little traffic. **Road 1**, which circumnavigates the country for about 850 miles, is well signposted and mostly tarmac (although a few sections remain unpaved); ideally you need a week or two to explore properly. Most wildlife hotspots are within easy reach of this road, although many side roads are gravel and so much slower.

Ferries and short flights are needed to access certain locations, such as Grimsey and the Westman Islands. There are regular **bus services** between towns and villages, and a variety of day trips from Reykjavík. However, to get off the beaten track and spend quality time with wildlife it is much better to drive.

The standard of **accommodation** is generally high, and a wide range is available including official campsites. Make reservations as far in advance as possible.

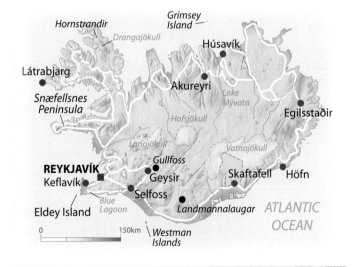

one million birds (some say two million) nest here in the extreme north-west of the country, including black-legged kittiwakes, northern fulmars, puffins, and common, Brünnich's and black guillemots. It is also home to the largest continuous razorbill colony in the world.

Grímsey Island

Lying right on the Arctic Circle, and the most northerly point of Iceland, this small island has a human population of fewer than 100 people. Its seabird population, however, is numbers in the hundreds of thousands. Arctic terns, puffins, razorbills and common, Brünnich's and black guillemots are all common. I've also seen blue, fin, humpback and minke whales from shore.

Húsavík

This quaint town in north-east Iceland has a picturesque harbour and long-distance views of snow-capped peaks. But it is best known for whale watching. During summer, three-hour trips into Skjálfandi Bay regularly encounter humpbacks, minkes, white-beaked dolphins and harbour porpoises. Blue whales are seen on many trips too, especially in June and early July. Fin whales, sei whales, orcas, long-finned pilot whales and other species turn up from time to time. The Húsavík Whale Museum is well worth a visit.

Leaping with
LEMURS
Madagascar

You can't say 'Madagascar is like somewhere-or-other' because, simply, it isn't. There is nowhere else on the planet like this beguiling wildlife wonderland

Bad omen:
The aesthetically
challenged aye-aye
is still considered
a portent of evil by
some local people

The experience

What? A jaw-dropping assemblage of weird and wonderful wildlife you can't see anywhere else

Where? The island of Madagascar, in the Indian Ocean

How? Fly to the capital, Antananarivo; travel by air, boat or 4WD, and explore on foot

P art African and part South-East Asian, Madagascar is the kind of place that grabs you by the scruff of the neck and shakes you about until you fall head over heels in love with its unique and consummate charm. It happened to me and it's happened to everyone else I know who has been there.

When it decided to slip away from the ancient mega-continent of Gondwana some 160 million years ago, it unwittingly made a good tactical move. The new island, roughly the size of France, travelled a couple of hundred miles east before settling off the coast of southern Africa. There, while the rest of the world grappled with the emergence of *Homo sapiens*, it was able to develop completely unscathed. And while all the less fortunate creatures left behind on the African mainland ultimately faced a barrage of competition from the

Above: Giant Grandidier baobabs line the road at Baobab Alley

Right: A ring-tailed lemur is one of Madagascar's many must-see mammals

likes of monkeys, lions and woodpeckers, the inhabitants of Madagascar had the fourth-largest island in the world all to themselves.

Visiting this chip off the old Gondwana block is rather like landing on another planet. The plants and animals are vaguely familiar – they resemble monkeys, hedgehogs and civets, for example – yet they are actually lemurs, tenrecs and jabadys. What's happened is that in Madagascar evolution has come up with different solutions to the same problems elsewhere in the world.

This is what makes it so thrilling and stimulating (and important) from a wildlife point of view: virtually everything that lives here doesn't exist anywhere else. All in all, more than 80 percent of the wildlife inhabiting the 1,000-mile-long island – including every single native terrestrial mammal – is unique to Madagascar.

Unfortunately, the gigantic ostrich-like elephant birds, false aardvarks, dwarf

hippos, giant lemurs nearly as big as men, and a host of other startlingly different creatures have all disappeared since people arrived in Madagascar, less than 2,000 years ago. And with the human population doubling in the past 20 years alone, the destruction continues – worst of all, the forest that once clothed the island like a protective coat is disappearing fast, being chopped and burned down to provide more elbow room for agriculture.

But Madagascar is still stuffed full of wildlife goodies. The undisputed stars are lemurs, of course, and no fewer than 100 different species are currently recognized. Found nowhere else (apart from small populations of introduced mongoose and black lemurs in the nearby Comoros Islands), they range in size from diminutive mouse lemurs (the smallest primates in the world) to indris (the size of large monkeys).

There are two species on the top of everyone's wish-list: ring-tailed lemurs

and aye-ayes. With their distinctive black-and-white coats, soft-toy cuddliness and air of swaggering arrogance, ring-tailed lemurs are great fun to watch. Whereas aye-ayes are just plain weird – undoubtedly among the strangest, most enigmatic and most endearing animals on the planet.

But whether it is lemurs you are after, or any of the other unique mammals, from fosas to tenrecs, or the myriad endemic birds, amphibians, reptiles and insects, Madagascar never disappoints.

Here are some of my own personal favourite sites (moving around the country anti-clockwise):

Andasibe-Mantadia National Park

This is one of the easiest parks to visit – it's a four-hour drive east from the capital – and is one of the most popular. It comprises two fabulous swathes of rainforest: Analamazoatra Special Reserve (more commonly known as Périnet) and the

Getting its groove on: A diademed sifaka appears to dance (actually bouncing on its hind legs) across open ground at Mantadia NP

Below: A researcher holds a giant jumping rat at Kirindy Forest; the quiet shores of Nosy Mangabé; the smallest primate in the world, a Madame Berthe's mouse lemur in Kirindy Forest

SPECIES CHECKLIST

- Aye-aye
- Indri
- Ring-tailed lemur
- Madame Berthe's mouse lemur
- Brown mouse lemur
- Grey mouse lemur
- Grey-brown mouse lemur
- Greater bamboo lemur
- White-footed sportive lemur
- Eastern fork-marked lemur
- Diademed sifaka
- Coquerel's sifaka
- Verreaux's sifaka
- Red-fronted brown lemur
- White-fronted brown lemur
- Black-and-white ruffed lemur
- Red-ruffed lemur
- Fosa
- Jabady (striped civet)
- Giant jumping rat
- Greater hedgehog tenrec
- Madagascar fruit bat
- Humpback whale
- Madagascar coucal
- Red-breasted coua
- Coquerel's coua
- White-headed vanga
- Madagascar serpent eagle
- Madagascar harrier hawk
- Spider tortoise
- Panther chameleon
- Pygmy chameleon
- Leaf-tailed gecko
- Madagascar boa
- Green-backed mantella frog
- Grandidier's baobab

… and many more

"It's possible to see as many as ten different lemur species in a couple of days and nights; it's also outstanding for bird watching"

less-often visited Mantadia National Park. It's *the* hotspot for indri – two groups have been habituated to people – and excellent sightings are virtually guaranteed. But it is possible to see as many as ten different lemur species in a couple of days and nights here: it is very good for diademed sifakas and black-and-white ruffed lemurs, for example, and is one place where a lucky few get to see greater bamboo lemurs (one of the rarest lemurs in the world). It is also outstanding for bird watching, and has a good selection of reptiles and amphibians.

Vakona Forest Lodge has its own 'Lemur Island' with a number of habituated lemurs, which is well worth a visit. It is a great place for photography, with a diademed sifaka that dances on the path, black-and-white ruffed lemurs feeding from your hand, grey bamboo lemurs leaping from tree to tree, and brown lemurs climbing all over your head.

There are several hotels and lodges on the doorstep. The park is open year-round, but the best months to visit are April, May and September to December.

Aye-aye Island (Île Roger)

A handful of aye-ayes were introduced to this 75-acre island on the Mananara River years ago, and it is now the easiest place to see them in Madagascar (although, strictly speaking, they aren't truly wild). After a short boat trip from the outskirts of Mananara, you are taken by a guide along a well-worn path through secondary forest (this was once a coconut, banana and lychee plantation) to the animals' favourite trees, and then wait until nightfall. They are seen, by torchlight, pretty much every night. Other lemurs introduced to the island include Masaola woolly lemur and white-fronted brown and eastern grey bamboo lemurs.

It is difficult to get to Mananara by road, but there is an airstrip and you can get a flight from Maroantsetra or Toamasina. There is a delightfully ramshackle hotel within a stone's throw of the airstrip. Try to avoid the wet cyclone season, from January to March.

Nosy Mangabé Special Reserve

This idyllic tropical island, in Antongil Bay off the north-east coast, was once believed to be the last place on earth where aye-ayes could be found (although they have been discovered elsewhere on the mainland since). It's still the best place to see a wild aye-aye. If you had to be stranded on a desert island then this would be the one to go for. With beautiful sandy coves, waterfall grottos, extravagant trees complete with huge buttress roots and hung with strangler figs and orchids, it is cloaked in lowland rainforest from the water's edge to its 1,100-foot peak. It is absolutely bursting with wildlife: white-fronted brown lemurs, black-and-white ruffed lemurs, brown mouse lemurs, greater hedgehog tenrecs, panther chameleons, leaf-tailed geckos, Madagascar tree boas, green-backed mantella frogs, and much, much more. It is also a haven for the crème de la crème of chameleons – the pygmy chameleon, one of the smallest in the world. There are also breeding humpback whales in the bay between July and September.

Get a boat from Maroantsetra (depending on the vessel, it takes about 30-40 minutes). You can do a day trip, but don't miss out on such a beautiful place (you need to be there overnight to see aye-ayes and much of the other wildlife). There is a pleasant campsite at the back of

My best day

I'll never forget one particular morning in Andasibe-Mantadia National Park. I was woken at 5am sharp by an eerie, wailing sound as loud as a fire alarm. It was dawn chorus with a difference – the territorial songs of huge teddy-bear-faced lemurs, called indris. I leapt out of bed in a half-conscious heart-pumping panic, got up in the dark and spent the rest of the morning following them up and down the wet, spongy, steep, forested slopes. It's the babies I remember most. They were pure entertainment – no word has been invented to describe cuteness on such a grandiose scale – and looked permanently wide-eyed and surprised as they bounced from branch to branch like rubber yo-yos.

the beach, with covered tent platforms. Try to avoid the wet cyclone season, from January to March.

Masaola National Park

On the north-east coast, this is the largest protected area in Madagascar. It contains a vast expanse of lowland rainforest, as well as mangrove swamps and 40 square miles of marine reserves.

Masaola is particularly good for red-ruffed lemur, white-fronted brown lemur and eastern fork-marked lemur (the latter on night walks), but it is also possible to see western grey bamboo lemur, Masaola woolly lemur, hairy-eared dwarf lemur, brown-tailed mongoose, helmet and Bernier's vangas, Madagascar serpent eagle, Madagascar red owl, stump-tailed leaf chameleon, several species of gecko (gold dust day, Madagascar day and leaf-tailed), and much more. There are breeding humpback whales in Antongil Bay from July to September.

There are two ways to get to the park: by boat from Maroantsetra or by car from Antalaha. There is some good snorkelling in the marine reserves, or try exploring by kayak. There are some good campsites on the peninsula, and there is basic accommodation in surrounding villages. This is an exceptionally wet part of the country, and it rains much of the year, but try to avoid the cyclone season from January to March. The best time is from September to December.

Ankarana Special Reserve

Ankarana is reputed to have one of the highest desnsities of primates anywhere in the world. Some of the species found here include: crowned lemur, Sanford's brown

"On Berenty Private Reserve, the ring-tailed lemur is impossible to miss – intimate encounters are virtually guaranteed"

lemur, Ankarana sportive lemur, northern rufous mouse lemur and Amber Mountain fork-marked lemur. It is also a good spot for fosa, jabady and greater hedgehog tenrec, as well as panther and white-lipped chameleons. Located near a limestone massif, the reserve is well known for its impressive (and almost impenetrable) landscape formed of karst pinnacles, or 'tsingy'. A network of nearly 100 miles of subterranean rivers and caves is home to Madagascar's largest eel, a blind shrimp found nowhere else, and Nile crocodiles.

Ankarana is only accessible in the dry season (May to November). You need a four-wheel drive to get there, from Antsiranana (Diego Suarez), or go in on foot. There is accommodation available in Mahamasina, or you can camp in the reserve. The best time to visit is from late April to November, which is the area's dry season.

Below: Cat or mongoose? The classification of the fosa – as spotted in the Kirindy Forest – has kept biologists arguing for years

Kirindy Forest Reserve

This dry deciduous forest reserve in western Madagascar is not as rich as some of the eastern rainforests, but it is home to a lot of endemic and endangered animals.

Kirindy is the best place to see fosa, the largest carnivore in Madagascar; looking like a cross between a puma and a mongoose (actually, it's more like an Egyptian carving of a sacred cat), there is nothing else quite like it. It is also a hotspot for Verreaux's sifaka – these black-faced, creamy-white lemurs are easy to spot and sometimes prance along the ground on their hind legs. It is the only place in the world to see Madame Berthe's mouse lemur, which is the smallest of all the world's primates. It is also the only place to see the giant jumping rat, which is roughly the size of a small cat and looks like a rabbit with a horse's head. But that's just the tip of the iceberg – Kirindy has a host of other wildlife. Much is nocturnal, so be prepared for torch-lit walks and late nights (it is probably the premier nocturnal site in Madagascar).

The reserve is a bumpy three-hour drive from Morondava. There are several simple bungalows and a communal dormitory, and basic camping facilities. By far the best time for wildlife is October to April although this is during the rainy season (October is relatively dry but at other times during the rains road conditions can be difficult – especially mid-January to late March – and it gets very hot from November onwards).

Don't forget to stop off en route at the famous Baobab Alley, two parallel lines of statuesque giant Grandidier's baobabs. Quite unlike trees in lesser parts of the world, they have massively swollen trunks (giving them the shape of giant Chianti bottles) festooned with sparse and ridiculously stubby and twisty branches.

Berenty Private Reserve

This small, private reserve is famous for its friendly ring-tailed lemurs and is the best

Keep up: The speedy ring-tailed lemurs of Berenty are bundles of energy

Need to know

WHEN TO GO

November to March is the hot, wet summer season; **April to October** is the cooler, dry winter season (when it's very cold at night in the central highlands and the capital). However, the amount of rain does vary enormously from year to year and from region to region. Generally, the **best months to visit are April to early November** (though this does vary from place to place – see the hotspots for more information). **Avoid August and Christmas**, which can be busy. The worst time is mid-January to March, when torrential rainfall can make some roads all but impassable and cyclones are likely in the east and north-east.

HOW TO DO IT

Fly to Antananarivo (via Paris, Johannesburg, Nairobi, Mauritius, Réunion or several cities in South-East Asia). There are many different ways to explore the country. There are luxury hotels, for people who like their creature comforts; or you can join an expedition cruise ship and avoid the challenges of overland travel. Alternatively, there are lots of **naturalist-led, organised tours**, staying in reasonable hotels or camping. It is also relatively easy to travel independently, using the famous taxi-brousses (mini-buses or converted vans) to get around (or tracteur-brousses, if conditions get tough). It is still possible to have a genuine adventure in Madagascar and it's **not difficult to venture off the beaten track**.

Travelling around the country usually involves a range of transport: scheduled and charter flights, a motley collection of boats, and 4WD cars or coaches. In many areas, the **so-called roads can be challenging and slow**. There are few railway lines, and they are mostly for cargo. The track between Fianarantsoa and Manakara, on the east coast, is the only one that regularly takes passengers. There are also opportunities to dive, kayak, cycle and rock-climb in many parts of the country.

Bear in mind that Madagascar is not the most efficient country in the world. But that's part of its charm – you just have to **go with the right attitude** and make the most of it.

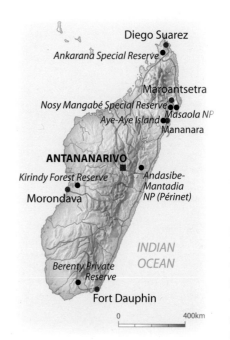

place in Madagascar to see them. Located close to the Mandrare River, it is home to natural gallery forest and semi-arid spiny forest (yet surrounded by a gargantuan sisal plantation). It is a slightly surreal place, with bright-red sandy roads, white picket fences and the kind of chalets you'd expect to find on Chesil Beach. But with a comfortable lodge and an excellent network of paths and forest trails, it is an easy place to visit. The ring-tails are impossible to miss and intimate encounters are virtually guaranteed. It is also a great place for Verreaux's sifaka (it's *the* place to see them 'dancing' across open ground), as

well as red-fronted brown lemur, white-footed sportive lemur, grey mouse lemur, grey-brown mouse lemur, Madagascar fruit bat, and radiated and spider tortoises.

Located on the southern tip of Madagascar, Berenty is a two- or three-hour drive (or slalom – it's a very windy, potholed, bumpy road) from Fort Dauphin. The only place to stay is Berenty Lodge, inside the reserve. It is open year-round, though the ring-tailed lemurs give birth in September or October (at the end of the dry season); the youngsters are weaned in February or March. The exceedingly hot, dry season is November to February.

Creating a buzz:
Hummingbirds can
beat their wings up to
70 times a second

Hovering with
HUMMINGBIRDS

Arizona: Huachuca Mountains

I may spend much of my time with the leviathans of the animal world, but these record-breaking, fast-living little birds always take my breath away

The experience

What? Being enthralled by as many as 15 different species of hummingbird

Where? High in the mountains of south-eastern Arizona, close to the Mexican border

How? Sit quietly next to some flowers or sugar-water feeders, and marvel

There are approximately 330 species of hummingbirds throughout North, Central and South America. The closer you get to the equator, the more species you encounter: Ecuador, for example, is home to about half of all known species. North America doesn't have the greatest diversity, but it does have more opportunities for watching these remarkable little birds than other parts of the world.

The hotspot is the south-west, along the US-Mexico border from western Texas through southern New Mexico to southern Arizona. It sometimes seems that every other house in this corner of the United States has sugar-water feeders (looking like upside-down jam-jars) hanging somewhere on the porch or in the backyard. In a week of birding in the mountains and deserts of south-eastern

"Hummers hovered in front of me – I could feel their wings against my cheeks; suddenly, one put its beak right inside my mouth and drank"

My best day

It was the first time I had ever worn make-up – let alone bright red lipstick – and I looked like Jack Lemmon in *Some Like It Hot*. With a crowd of onlookers egging me on, I puckered my colourful lips and pointed them towards the sky. The plan was for the hummingbirds to mistake them for their favourite nectar-giving flowers, and I had a mouthful of sickly sweet sugar-water just in case. Within seconds there were several 'hummers' hovering right in front of me and I could feel their wingbeats against my cheeks. Suddenly, one put its beak right inside my mouth – and drank. Wildlife encounters don't get much closer than that.

SPECIES CHECKLIST

- Anna's hummingbird
- Costa's hummingbird
- Black-chinned hummingbird
- Broad-billed hummingbird
- Blue-throated hummingbird
- Magnificent hummingbird
- Rufous hummingbird
- Lucifer hummingbird
- Violet-crowned hummingbird
- Berylline hummingbird
- Broad-tailed hummingbird
- White-eared hummingbird
- Allen's hummingbird
- Calliope hummingbird
- Plain-capped starthroat

Arizona, in particular, it's possible to see as many as 15 different hummingbird species – more than anywhere else in the United States. Almost half of the hummingbird species found here are rare, or unheard of, elsewhere in the country.

One of the best places is Beatty's Guest Ranch in south-eastern Arizona, some 5,800 feet up in the mountains, with the Mexican border just a few miles away and a spectacular view down a valley to the desert below. According to the Southeastern Arizona Bird Observatory, this is the hottest hummingbird-watching spot in the entire state. You stay in snug rustic cabins on the edge of a forest, and can watch hummingbirds right outside your bedroom window.

I will never forget pulling back the curtains on my very first morning at the ranch. There were hummingbirds everywhere. Most of the time they were little more than blurred shapes, like bees on speed, whizzing backwards and

forwards past the window. Sometimes they paused in front of the sugar-water to feed, either perching or hovering with the immaculate precision of experienced helicopter pilots. I saw no fewer than 11 species before breakfast, including black-chinned, magnificent, blue-throated and broad-tailed. It is possible to see 15 species at the ranch altogether, including rarities such as white-eared, lucifer and berylline hummingbirds. Literally thousands of them arrive on the ranch during spring and stay throughout the summer; many others pass through on migration.

Hanging from trees, bushes, fences and buildings, there are dozens of hummingbird feeders full of a magic potion (four parts water to one part white sugar) that is designed to replicate the natural nectar of hummingbird flowers. The owners of the ranch keep these feeders topped up throughout the day and get through a mind-boggling 1,100lbs of sugar (imagine 550 two-pound bags) every year.

With the fastest wingbeats of all birds (up to 70 beats a second in most North American species) and an ability to hover for up to an hour non-stop, hummingbirds need a continuous supply of fuel. This is why they drink huge quantities of energy-rich nectar – and sugar-water. Living life on the edge, they can never be far from their next meal.

The different species are unbelievably difficult to tell apart. The problem is that hummingbirds are the chameleons of the bird world: they actually change colour right in front of your eyes. As they move around in relation to the sun, their bright, iridescent hues seem to wink on and off.

A rufous hummingbird, for instance, can look fiery-red head-on, but as it turns the colour shifts to orange, yellow, blackish-brown and ultimately green. Changing appearance makes sense, biologically: if a male wants to impress a female he shows his best side, but if he wants to hide from a predator he merely turns away and almost disappears amongst the foliage.

Identity parade: Their ever-changing iridescent plumage makes it tricky to tell hummingbird species apart. This is a broad-billed hummingbird; and it's a black-chinned opposite

Need to know

WHEN TO GO

Small numbers of hummingbirds are resident year-round in south-east Arizona, but thousands more **arrive in early spring** and stay **until early autumn**, when they leave for warmer climes further south. The best time for local breeders is late April to the end of July, but numbers swell considerably with migrants and vagrants in April/May and August/September. The peak time for both numbers and species is usually **August**. Rare Allen's hummingbirds are most often seen in July and plain-capped starthroats June to August.

The seasons for **other North American hotspots** are different: the Gulf Coast is best August/September then November to late February; the Rocky Mountain Flyway from March to September (best July and August); the Pacific Flyway is best mid-February to late April along the coast, and June to late September in the coastal plain and mountains; the Atlantic Flyway is best late July to early September; the Mississippi Flyway is best July to September.

HOW TO DO IT

Thousands of hummingbirds descend on **Beatty's Miller Canyon Guest Ranch**, near Sierra Vista, every year. There are cabins for rent (each with their own feeders), and limited space for tents and small RVs. **Day visitors are welcome** (with limited access) for a small fee.

Other good sites in the area include: Ash Canyon, just south of Miller Canyon; Paton's Hummingbird Haven, on the edge of Patagonia-Sonoita Creek Preserve (most reliable site in the USA for violet-crowned hummingbirds); Santa Rita Lodge, Madera Canyon (crowded at weekends); Madera Kubo Cabins, Madera Canyon (also the best place in the US to see flame-coloured tanagers); Cave Creek Canyon, near Portal in the Chiricahua Mountains (good for burrowing owls and pronghorn); and Ramsey Canyon Preserve.

Southeastern Arizona Bird Observatory, in Bisbee, allows visitors to watch experts capture, ring, weigh, measure and release hummingbirds as part of a long-term study. Or try **volunteering** for The Hummingbird Monitoring Network.

Trying to make a positive identification in a hurry, before the bird turns into a blur and helicopters away, is all part of the fun. Yet the experts can identify hummingbirds with their eyes closed – simply by the distinctive sounds of their minuscule wingbeats. Broad-tailed hummingbirds, for example, have a metallic trill to their wingbeats; male black-chinned hummingbirds make a dull, flat whine.

Visitors to the ranch spend hour after happy hour sitting watching dozens, sometimes hundreds, of these charismatic little birds stocking up on the ready supply of fuel. It's an extraordinary – and enlightening – experience. If, like me, you had always imagined them to be easy-going Tinkerbells, think again. Far from being all sweetness and light, they are miniature fighter pilots: small Samurai warriors, squabbling and fighting in their determination to keep the competition away from their favourite flowers or feeders. They've even been known to attack much larger birds in momentary fits of bad temper.

As a researcher from the Southeastern Arizona Bird Observatory once noted: if hummingbirds were the size of ravens, no one would be safe walking in the woods.

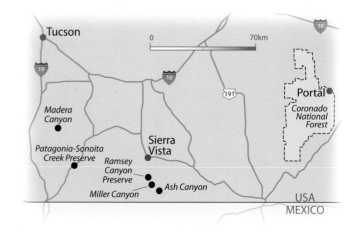

Counting
PENGUINS
& SEALS

South Atlantic Ocean: South Georgia

With 50 million seabirds and more than five million seals crammed onto an island the size of Essex, it's impossible to exaggerate the sheer wonder of remote and beautiful South Georgia

Regal riot: Try counting king penguins on the beaches of South Georgia

The experience

What? Mingling with some of the largest concentrations of wildlife on the planet

Where? The sub-Antarctic island where Shackleton sailed to get help

How? A comfortable expedition cruise aboard a ship with an ice-strengthened hull

A mere speck in the immensity of the Southern Ocean, South Georgia is remote by any standards. Antarctica, South America and Africa are about 930 miles, 1,300 miles and 2,980 miles away, respectively, while even the Falkland Islands are a distant 870 miles.

Strictly-speaking, South Georgia is a sub-Antarctic island. But its harsh climate, rugged, mountainous terrain and the sheer abundance of seals, penguins and petrels – as well as an embracing sweep of the Polar Front – make it decidedly Antarctic in character. Buffeted by fierce, unpredictable storms and thrashed by choppy seas, it has an ethereal beauty that is nothing short of breathtaking. Sharp, snow-capped mountains rise to a height of 9,626 feet and run like a dragon's spine down the length of the island; steep,

Above: You never forget the first time you catch sight of South Georgia; black-browed-albatrosses and other seabirds follow the ship; finding enough space to park a Zodiac amongst all the wildlife can be a challenge

towering cliffs plummet straight into the sea; permanent ice and snow cover more than half of the island; it is encircled by a flotilla of rugged offshore islets and rocks; and there are no trees.

There is no permanent human population on South Georgia, although there are small teams of British Antarctic Survey scientists on Bird Island and in Grytviken, the only real settlement in the area. Yet there is an indescribable aura about the place, perhaps because it is steeped in an extraordinary history of violence, destruction, greed, adventure, courage and sacrifice.

The first person to step ashore was Captain James Cook, on 17 January 1775, who claimed and named the island for King George III. Cook didn't like South Georgia at all: it is a land, he said, "doomed by Nature to perpetual frigidness: never to feel the warmth of the sun's rays; whose horrible and savage aspects I have not words to describe."

But he returned with stories of seals as far as the eye could see – and set off a stampede of sealers taking fur seal skins and elephant seal oil. So many of the animals were slaughtered that, by the 1930s, no more than a few hundred were left. Thankfully, they have made an astounding recovery in the decades since.

Unfortunately, the same can't be said for whales. No fewer than 175,250 of them were slaughtered around South Georgia between 1904 and 1965, when the industry was abandoned because there were so few seals left. One particular female blue whale, landed at Grytviken in 1909, measured 110 feet 2 inches – the largest animal ever recorded.

The person who will always be inextricably linked with South Georgia is Ernest Shackleton, of course. His first visit was in November 1914, aboard the *Endurance*, when he intended to make the first trans-Antarctic crossing. It's a famous story – his ship was crushed in the ice, he

returned to South Georgia in May 1916 in the tiny *James Caird*, and with Frank Worsley and Tom Crean completed the first island crossing in his determination to get help. Shackleton died of a heart attack on 5 January 1922, shortly after arriving in South Georgia on yet another expedition. He was buried in the whalers' cemetery, in Grytviken, according to his wishes.

Wildlife of South Georgia

But it's the wildlife that most people visit South Georgia to see. This small island, 106 miles long and 19 miles wide in the middle, is home to the greatest density of wildlife on the planet. The surrounding seas are teeming with krill, squid, fish and other marine life, which provide a super-abundance of food for penguins, albatrosses, seals, whales and all the other animals higher up the food chain.

There are more than 50 million breeding seabirds and more than five million seals, so the numbers speak for themselves. Among

The Boss: Antarctic fur seals rule the beaches of South Georgia and will not hesitate to drive off human interlopers

SPECIES CHECKLIST

- Southern right whale
- Humpback whale
- Fin whale
- Dwarf minke whale
- Sperm whale
- Killer whale
- Long-finned pilot whale
- Hourglass dolphin
- Southern elephant seal
- Antarctic fur seal
- Weddell seal
- King penguin
- Macaroni penguin
- Chinstrap penguin
- Gentoo penguin
- Wandering albatross
- Black-browed albatross
- Light-mantled sooty albatross
- Grey-headed albatross
- Antarctic prion
- Fairy prion
- Wilson's storm petrel
- Black-bellied storm petrel
- Common diving-petrel
- White-chinned petrel
- South Georgia diving-petrel
- Northern giant petrel
- Southern giant petrel
- Cape petrel
- Snow petrel
- Blue petrel
- Snowy sheathbill
- Brown skua
- Kelp gull
- Antarctic tern
- South Georgia shag
- South Georgia pintail
- South Georgia pipit
- … and many more

> ## "The small island of South Georgia – 106 miles long and no more than 19 miles wide – is home to the greatest density of wildlife on the planet"

them are 22 million Antarctic prions, as many as eight million common diving-petrels, several million macaroni penguins, and two million white-chinned petrels. South Georgia is a critical breeding ground for other seabirds, too. One-fifth of the world population of wandering albatrosses – about 1,500 pairs – nests around the island. Watching the spectacular courtship display of the bird with the longest wingspan in the world is an unforgettable experience. But as with all albatrosses, numbers have been declining worldwide due to the phenomenal impact of longline fishing, so the breeding colonies are thinner than they used to be.

The island can even claim the world's most southerly passerine, or perching bird – the South Georgia pipit – which is found nowhere else in the world. The South Georgia pintail, a sub-species of the yellow-billed pintail, is also endemic.

There are no native land mammals, although about 20 reindeer were introduced from Norway between 1911 and 1925 and they have thrived in the absence of predators. There is now a population of over 3,000 animals.

But it's the seals that are so utterly overwhelming. South Georgia is the breeding ground for no fewer than 4.5 million Antarctic fur seals (95% of the entire world population) and more than 500,000 southern elephant seals (half the world population). Some fur seal breeding beaches are so crammed full that it is

Right: One of South Georgia's 500,000 southern elephant seals takes a well-earned break; Grytviken and its abandoned whaling station; no fewer than 175,250 whales were slaughtered around South Georgia in just 60 years

Below: The gravestone of legendary explorer and adventurer Sir Ernest Shackleton

impossible to land on them without causing huge disruption and risking an incident: territorial bulls will not hesitate to drive off human interlopers and have a nasty bite. But you can watch them from the safety of Zodiacs or, in other areas, carefully pick your way through the throng. The elephant seals are easier-going, but no less impressive. Watching the bulls – the largest seals in the world – fighting over their harems is an electrifying wildlife spectacle, packed with tension and drama.

There is wildlife everywhere and, far from bolting in the opposite direction every time a person appears on the scene, most of the animals here merely stand and stare – or come and take a closer look.

Nowhere on South Georgia is disappointing to visit, but here are a few of my favourite hotspots (moving from north to south):

Elsehul

A picturesque cove at the north-western extremity of South Georgia, Elsehul is packed with a remarkable abundance of wildlife and is a great place for Zodiac cruising. There are so many fur seals here between November and late January – more than almost anywhere else in South Georgia – that the beaches are a writhing mass and landings are impossible. It is also good for elephant seals, especially early in the season.

Elsehul is a breeding ground for two species of penguin (macaroni and gentoo

– there is also a group of moulting king penguins), three albatrosses (black-browed, grey-headed and light-mantled sooty), giant petrels, blue-eyed shags and sheathbills. It is also a good place to see white-chinned petrels, cape petrels, Wilson's storm petrels, brown skuas, Antarctic terns and even wandering albatrosses and South Georgia pintails.

Prion Island

Prion Island is an important breeding site for wandering albatrosses. Several dozen pairs of these magnificent birds nest on the tiny island (it's only about half a mile long) in a typical year. It is also one of the best

places to see South Georgia pipits, which occur all over the island. It has large numbers of breeding common diving-petrels, white-chinned petrels, southern and northern giant petrels, and Antarctic prions. Light-mantled sooty albatrosses and South Georgia pintails also breed here.

Elephant seals breed, too, but from November to January the main landing beach is dominated by breeding fur seals.

Hercules Bay

This is one of the best places in South Georgia to see macaroni penguins. Zodiac cruises along the shore are great fun and usually offer the best sightings. Named after the Norwegian whaling ship, *Hercules*, this beautiful site is also home to light-mantled sooty albatrosses, white-chinned petrels, southern giant petrels and blue-eyed shags. The shingle beach is lined with elephant seals and fur seals, and a small herd of reindeer appears from time to time.

Stromness Harbour

An historic site with reindeer, elephant seals, fur seals and gentoo penguins thrown in for good measure. It is where Shackleton, Worsley and Crean walked into the now-derelict whaling station, after their voyage in the *James Caird* in 1916. It was a major whaling base until as recently as 1961.

It is a great place for watching fur seal pups because, in January and February, hundreds of them gather to play in the shallows of the river mouth. Several hundred elephant seals breed and moult here, too, and it is one of the best places to see reindeer, which sometimes wander among the whaling station buildings. There are several small colonies of gentoo penguins in the vicinity and there is a large colony of Antarctic terns in the hills behind the whaling station.

It is possible to hike to Stromness from Fortuna Bay. The so-called Shackleton Walk, which retraces the steps of Shackleton, Worsley and Crean on the final

"The colour, the noise, the smell and the commotion of this extraordinary spectacle guarantees sensory overload at every turn"

leg of their rescue mission, is less than four miles – but much of it is steep and on slippery scree slopes, so it is not for the faint-hearted.

Grytviken

This is the most regularly visited site on the island and there is a lot to see. Set amid spectacular scenery, with snow-capped mountains and glaciers forming a beautiful backdrop even by South Georgia standards, Grytviken is home to an abandoned whaling station, the wonderful South Georgia Museum, the Whaler's Church and Ernest Shackleton's grave.

This is also a good place for wildlife. South Georgia pintails are a highlight, but the surrounding mountains are also superb for a wide variety of breeding seabirds. They harbour Wilson's, white-chinned and black-bellied storm petrels, South Georgian diving-petrels, light-mantled sooty albatrosses, giant petrels, kelp gulls and Antarctic terns (although many of these are best seen at dusk). King penguins stand around in solemn groups, moulting, and there are elephant seals and fur seals all around the bay.

St. Andrew's Bay

This is a real showstopper – a highlight of any visit to South Georgia. Against a phenomenal mountainous backdrop, king penguins crowd the beach in numbers that will take your breath away. The colour, the noise, the smell and the commotion of this extraordinary spectacle guarantees sensory overload at every turn. It is all a bit overwhelming, especially on a gorgeous sunny spring day, so find a quiet spot and simply sit to drink it all in.

King penguins breed prolifically on South Georgia. There are believed to be as many as 500,000 breeding pairs on the island altogether, in 34 different rookeries. St. Andrews is the largest, with more than 150,000 pairs. It is also home to at least 6,000 southern elephant seals – more than any other beach on the island – and they are literally everywhere during October and November.

The kings here have a staggered 18-month-long breeding cycle, so the rookeries are full of birds year-round. It is often possible to watch every stage in a single day – adults incubating eggs or feeding chicks of different ages, as well as young penguins in their crèches.

The other top spot for king penguins is Salisbury Plain, which has the second largest rookery with at least 60,000 pairs. During the moult period, there have been reports of as many as 250,000 birds on the black-sand beach at once.

Landing at both St. Andrew's and Salisbury can be difficult due to large waves, though, and visits are very dependent on sea and weather conditions.

Gold Harbour

Widely regarded as one of the most beautiful places in South Georgia – which

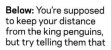

Below: You're supposed to keep your distance from the king penguins, but try telling them that

Festival of kings: St. Andrew's Bay resembles an avian Glastonbury – 150,000 penguin pairs breed here

Need to know

WHEN TO GO

The South Georgia tourist season runs from **October to February** (the southern spring and summer). The temperature at this time of year typically ranges from about 0°C (32°F) to 10°C (50°F) but can be considerably warmer or colder. Early in the season is best for ice and pristine snow. **Male elephant seals** are fighting from late August until mid-November; females come ashore to pup in September and October; they spend the rest of season onshore moulting: youngsters first, then females, then bulls. Fur seals pup in late November to late December; males have departed by mid-January; females visit the pups on and off for the remainder of the season. **King penguins** are present and breeding throughout. **Macaroni** penguins arrive in late October, lay their eggs a month later and are feeding chicks from the end of December. **Wandering albatrosses** are present and have chicks throughout; other albatrosses arrive in late September and October, and are feeding chicks from early January onwards.

HOW TO DO IT

Expedition cruise ships leave **Ushuaia, southern Argentina**, and combine the Antarctic Peninsula and the Falkland Islands with a few days at South Georgia. There are trips that explore South Georgia exclusively (these often leave from the Falkland Islands, which are just two or three days' sail away). Visitors are **not permitted to stay overnight** on the island. **Access to some areas are prohibited**, including several islets: Cooper Island, off the south-east; Annenkov Island, off the south; and Bird Island, off the north-west.

The south coast faces the prevailing westerly winds and tends to be generally inhospitable. The **north coast is more benign**, with many safe anchorages. In total, there are about 40 sites along the north coast that can be visited by tourists. These include: Elsehul, Salisbury Plain, King Edward Point, Prion Island, Prince Olav Harbour, Fortuna Bay, Hercules Bay, Leith Harbour, Stromness, Husvik, Drygalski Fjord, Maiviken, Grytviken, Cobblers Cove, Godthul, Ocean Harbour, St. Andrew's Bay, Moltke Harbour, Will Point, Gold Harbour and Larsen Harbour.

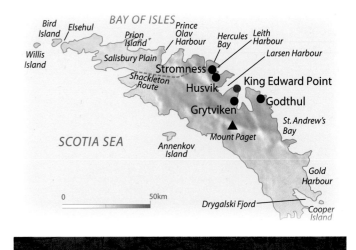

is saying something – Gold Harbour is home to a sizeable king penguin rookery (an estimated 25,000 pairs) as well as gentoo penguins, brown skuas, giant petrels, elephant seals and a few ubiquitous fur seals. There is a large Antarctic tern colony in the hills and a few light-mantled sooty albatrosses breed on the surrounding cliffs. It can also be a good location to view leopard seals, which sometimes visit to hunt penguins just offshore. The site consists of a sweeping beach with a mountainous and glacial backdrop and is particularly outstanding at dawn – the glorious colours created by the light giving the harbour its glamourous name.

Larsen Harbour

Larsen Harbour is home to South Georgia's only breeding Weddell seals. There aren't many of them – just a few dozen breeding females – and they have dispersed by mid-November, but individuals do appear from time to time throughout summer.

Larsen is also one of the premier breeding areas for snow petrels, which nest on the surrounding cliffs and mountain ledges and can be seen flying around with cape petrels. But there is a lot of other wildlife here, too, including Antarctic terns, South Georgia diving-petrels, Wilson's storm petrels, Antarctic prions and blue-eyed shags. There are even a few South Georgia pipits.

Might in shining armour: Greater
one-horned rhinos, with their grey,
plated skin, look positively prehistoric

Pointing at
PACHYDERMS

Assam, India: Kaziranga National Park

There are many great places to watch rhinos, but few much more magical than Kaziranga, where they're everywhere – and remarkably approachable

The experience

What? Getting up close and personal with greater one-horned rhinos and Asian elephants

Where? On the banks of the mighty Brahmaputra River, in the oldest national park in Assam

How? Go on safari by jeep or on elephant-back

Tucked away in the far north-eastern corner of India, halfway between Burma and Bhutan, Kaziranga is one of the greatest wildlife sanctuaries on earth. It is a beautiful park, set against the hazy backdrop of the Himalayas, with an astonishing variety of endangered wildlife, from sloth bears and capped langurs to leopards and western hoolock gibbons (the only apes in India).

A vast wilderness of more than 165 square miles, its signature habitat is exceedingly tall elephant grass, which can grow to a height of 20 feet. It also contains a mix of forest, reedbeds, marshes and shallow pools.

It lies on the southern bank of the Brahmaputra River and is defined by seasonal flooding: during the height of the monsoon, especially in July, August and early September, the river bursts its banks

and floods as much as 90% of the park. The wildlife survives by retreating to higher ground, in the Mikir Hills or on the Karbi Plateau.

Kaziranga's real claim to fame is its pachyderms: greater one-horned rhinos, in particular, and Asian elephants. It is also one of the most important strongholds in India for tigers.

When it was first established as a protected area, in 1905, the greater one-horned rhino population was at an all-time low of about a dozen. But intensive conservation efforts turned the tide and the first proper census, in 1966, counted 366 rhinos. Numbers have increased more than five-fold since then (2,048 at the last count, in 2009) and this dramatic recovery is widely regarded as one of the world's great conservation success stories.

It hasn't been easy – in the past century, more than 700 rhinos have been killed by poachers in Kaziranga. Although poaching has been brought under control, it is still a serious problem. It requires constant vigilance to keep the poachers at bay.

My best day

I'd been working on anti-poaching patrols for a couple of weeks, but had one free morning in Kaziranga before leaving – so joined an elephant-back safari for a final look at the park. As we trundled off into the tall grass, everywhere was cloaked in a magical early morning mist. We found tiger pug marks, saw a water buffalo and some elephants, passed several rhinos, and then stumbled upon a mother and her calf wallowing contentedly in a mud pool. The grand finale was a detour on the way back to Guwahati to see my favourite Ganges river dolphins, in the Kulsi River. You don't often see so many endangered species in a single day.

Home to an astonishing 70% of all the world's greater one-horned rhinos (the total population was estimated to be 2,913 in 2011), Kaziranga is absolutely fundamental to the survival of the species. Outside this (relatively) safe haven, there are small numbers in half a dozen other protected areas in India and about 530 individuals in Nepal.

Kaziranga is indisputably the best place to see them. And it's quite easy to get good views – especially from elephant-back – because the rhinos are used to people and don't seem to mind visitors getting up close and personal. Built like armoured tanks, with tough, gun-metal grey skin deeply folded into what look like series of overlapping plates, these formidable animals look decidedly prehistoric. A close encounter with a greater one-horned rhino feels like going back in time.

The park is also home to more than 1,000 Asian elephants, which are also quite approachable. I have seen as many as 200 together in a single herd, but fewer than 80 is more common. They tend to feed out in the open, early in the morning and late in the afternoon.

Pachyderm patrol: Kaziranga's greater one-horned rhinos and Asian elephants are, quite literally, the biggest draws

Below left: Endangered Ganges river dolphins can be seen in the local rivers

SPECIES CHECKLIST

- Asian elephant
- Greater one-horned rhino
- Tiger
- Leopard
- Jungle cat
- Fishing cat
- Sloth bear
- Asian black bear
- Asiatic water buffalo
- Indian gaur
- Swamp deer
- Sambar
- Barking deer
- Hog deer
- Indian wild boar
- Western hoolock gibbon
- Capped langur
- Assamese macaque
- Rhesus macaque
- Pangolin
- Ganges river dolphin
- Bengal florican
- Oriental honey buzzard
- Crested serpent eagle
- Pallas's fish eagle
- Grey-headed fish eagle
- Black-shouldered kite
- Brahminy kite
- Himalayan griffon vulture
- Greater adjutant stork
- Lesser adjutant stork
- Gharial

... and many more

Because Kaziranga is better known for its rhinos and elephants, its importance as a tiger stronghold is often forgotten. There are better places elsewhere in India to see these elusive and critically endangered big cats (Bandhavgarh National Park, in the heart of Madhya Pradesh, is probably the best) but Kaziranga harbours one of the highest concentrations of tigers anywhere in Asia. It's just that they are hard to see through all that thick elephant grass. There were 86 tigers in the park at the last count; with tiger numbers so precarious, and recent research showing a big reduction in their available habitat compared with just

"Home to an astonishing 70% of all the world's greater one-horned rhinos, Kaziranga is fundamental to the survival of the species"

Need to know

WHEN TO GO

Kaziranga National Park is open to visitors from roughly **mid-October to 30 April**. The best time to visit is from December onwards (the visibility is high after the annual grassland burning). Avoid Christmas and New Year, when it gets very busy. There are **three seasons**: **winter** (November to February, when it is cool at night, mild in the day, and

dry); **summer** (March to early May, when it is very hot and dry); and **monsoon** (late May to October, when the Brahmaputra River can break its banks at any time, and the park is closed to tourists).

HOW TO DO IT

From Delhi there are scheduled flights to **Guwahati**, the largest city in Assam, which is just over 135 miles from Kaziranga. There are buses from the city centre or you can hire a car and driver (the drive takes up to six hours). Alternatively, there are limited flights to **Jorhat**, which is only two hours' drive away from the park. It is also possible to **take a train** from Delhi or Calcutta (Kolkata) to Furkating, about two hours' drive away. Rhinos and elephants are often seen from the National Highway 37, which passes through the park. There are several lodges on the outskirts of the park, offering a variety of accommodation to suit all budgets.

All wildlife-watching is done from **open 4WD jeeps or on elephant-back**. Tours leave from the park headquarters in Kohora, always accompanied by park guides, and must be booked in advance. There are also several strategic **observation towers** open to visitors. Hiking is prohibited in Kaziranga itself, but there are limited opportunities nearby; you must walk with armed guards.

There are some excellent places to see **Ganges river dolphins**, on the Brahmaputra River itself and associated tributaries near Guwahati; Kulsi River, at Kukurmara, is particularly good. It is also worth visiting the **Hoollongapar Gibbon Wildlife Sanctuary**, which is 16 miles from Jorhat. This is a small reserve (only about eight square miles) but it has no fewer than **seven species of primate**: western hoolock gibbon, capped langur, Bengal slow loris, and stump-tailed, northern pig-tailed, rhesus and Assamese macaques. There are also small populations of Asian elephants and tigers, as well as wild boar, civet and over 200 species of birds.

---

a decade ago, a significant, well-protected population of this size is critical.

Kaziranga is also a good place to see wild Asiatic water buffalo. Although the domesticated version of this species is a familiar sight across India, the wild buffalo is one of the rarest mammals in India. With around 1,400 buffaloes, the park is home to more than half the world population (good news for the local tigers: they make perfect prey). In most parts of their limited range, water buffalo are shy and unapproachable – but they don't seem to be all that bothered by vehicles in Kaziranga and careful, close approaches are often possible.

Other wildlife here includes a rich array of birds, with about 500 species recorded to date. Kaziranga is renowned for birds of prey, in particular, but it is also a major winter visiting ground for many migratory species, lying as it does at the junction of the East Asian-Australasian Flyway and the Central Asian Flyway.

It also has two of the longest snakes in the world – the rock python and the reticulated python – as well as the longest venomous snake in the world, the king cobra. There are reputed to be lots of snakes in the park, although I have only ever seen one.

Eye to eye: Guadalupe's superb underwater visibility – 100ft or more – makes it the world's top great white site

Encountering GREAT WHITES

Mexico: Guadalupe Island

A week spent under water with the ultimate super-predator is simply too awe-inspiring to leave any room in your mind for fear

The experience

What? Cage-diving with the quintessential shark, the great white

Where? The remote island of Guadalupe, a tiny little dot in the North Pacific some 210 miles south-west of San Diego

How? From a live-aboard dive boat (no dive qualifications necessary)

Admittedly, it's an unusual way to spend your precious holiday. You fly to San Diego, in southern California, and take a small boat on a bumpy 20-hour rollercoaster ride to a remote volcanic island in the North Pacific. Then you jump overboard into cold water, with a giant tuna head for company, and hope for a close encounter with an animal many people would pay good money never to meet.

The great white shark's enormous size, powerful jaws, rows of large triangular teeth and jet-black eyes made it the perfect star of *Jaws* – the film that gave sharks such a terrible and undeserved reputation. But having met umpteen of these endangered animals over the years, I've not only emerged unscathed but also enjoyed some of my most impressive and unforgettable wildlife encounters.

My best day

One particular afternoon we had no fewer than five great whites, ranging in size from eight feet to more than 13 feet. The largest looked the size of a juggernaut from inside the cage, and kept racing towards us, mouth agape, before veering off at the last moment, usually only about two feet away from the end of my camera lens.

Once, it stuck its head right inside the cage, no more than a jagged, triangular tooth-length away. "How on earth can you top that?" I asked the others afterwards. "What can we possibly do next?" They looked amused. "I dunno," said the divemaster. "Maybe space travel?"

There are few places in the world where great white sharks are seen on a regular basis. The Western Cape, in South Africa, is best-known and has a prolific population of great whites. It is superb for surface watching – False Bay, in particular, is the best place for seeing great whites breach clear of the water – but underwater visibility is really poor compared to Guadalupe. Visibility is also a problem in the Farallon Islands, California, where it averages a mere 20 feet; however, surface watching can be dramatic, because this is where the sharks attack northern elephant seals at the surface. South Australia is the closest contender: the hotspot is the Neptune Islands, where visibility is highly variable but, on a good day, can rival Guadalupe.

In my experience, Guadalupe is best for underwater encounters. It has the advantage of being a seamount surrounded by deep blue water, which is why the visibility is so good – 100 feet is by no means unusual. It also has a well-deserved reputation for huge great whites:

the largest I have seen there was a 16-foot female, but others have reported individuals reaching 18 feet or more. And with as many as 100 great white sharks around the island in season, perhaps more, sightings are consistent. Suffice it to say, in shark-diving circles we talk about Guadalupe in hushed and reverential tones.

Until recently, it was better known for its seals. A century ago, Guadalupe was the last refuge of northern elephant seals and Guadalupe fur seals. Luckily, small numbers of both species managed to hide from sealers –otherwise, they would almost certainly have become extinct. There are also a number of interesting birds on the island, though they are hard to see without special permission to land. The rock wren, house finch and junco are all endemic sub-species, found only on Guadalupe.

But it's cage-diving with great whites that puts it on the wildlife map. When I first started visiting Guadalupe, the cages were more like a collection of wide open spaces. The gaps between the aluminium bars were plenty big enough for us to slip through into the sharks' world on the

SPECIES CHECKLIST

- Great white shark
- Northern elephant seal
- Guadalupe fur seal
- California sea lion
- Bottlenose dolphin
- Cuvier's beaked whale (occasional)
- Baird's beaked whale (occasional)
- Blue whale (sometimes en route)

outside and, as we discovered on several memorable occasions, were also plenty big enough for the sharks to slip through into our world on the inside. Nowadays, the cages are well and truly shark-proof (though you are still asked to sign an indemnity form, basically promising never to sue anyone about anything ever again, no matter what happens).

With the help of a special crane the cages are lifted off the deck and into the water at the back of the boat, while you get prepared. As well as a drysuit with plenty of warm layers underneath, you wear an exceptionally heavy weight belt or harness.

> "It stuck its head right inside the cage, no more than a jagged, triangular tooth-length away. 'How on earth can you top that?' I asked"

Pleased to meet you: Great white sharks may circle Guadalupe dive boats before they have even dropped anchor

Left: Guadalupe's great whites can reach up to 18ft long; cages typically hold four divers, who breathe through 'hookah line' air pipes

Need to know

WHEN TO GO

Great white shark trips are conducted mainly in **August, September and October**; although the sharks are usually present from the second half of July to at least January. Smaller males (10-13 feet) dominate earlier in the season, while larger females are more common later. **Water visibility** typically ranges from 80-120 feet (occasionally dropping down to as little as 20 feet for short periods). **Water temperature** averages 17-23°C/63-73°F; this can feel very cold when you spend long periods standing still in the shark cages. Guadalupe is remote, and open-ocean conditions prevail, but the island is large enough (98 square miles) to provide calm anchorages during inclement weather.

HOW TO DO IT

Guadalupe lies 150 miles off the Pacific coast of Baja California, in Mexico. The only way to get there is by **boat** and, since no-one is allowed ashore without special permission, shark divers must sleep on board (only a small number of fishermen and military personnel live on the island, which is a Biosphere Reserve). San Diego, in southern California, is the main gateway city (Ensenada, in Mexico, is secondary) and trips leave regularly during shark season. Most last five or six days, giving three or four days of cage-diving.

Most vessels carry two four-person **cages**, and 16 divers, so everyone rotates on an hourly basis. The cages are attached to the swim platform at the back of the boat and usually float just below the surface. There is a trapdoor in the roof so you simply drop inside and, weighed down by a heavy weight belt or harness, sink to the carpet of wire mesh on the bottom. Breathing is through a regulator attached to a 'hookah line', connected to air cylinders on the boat. **No dive qualifications are needed**, though you do need to be confident in the water.

Some operators use submersible cages to descend deeper into the sharks' world (typically about 30 feet) for a completely different perspective. You do need to be a qualified diver for this fantastic experience.

San Diego
Ensenada
USA
MEXICO
Baja California
Guadalupe Island
PACIFIC OCEAN
0   200km

I normally carry weights totalling 44 pounds (equivalent to strapping 22 bags of sugar to my waist) and stagger around the deck like an Olympic weightlifter. The aim is to be heavy enough to be able to stand firmly on the bottom of the cage, rather than floating around out of control.

Another change in the last few years is the amount of chum (blood, guts and fish oil) being used to attract the sharks. Huge amounts were considered essential in the past, but many operators have found that without chum – or with nothing more than a little fish oil – the sharks are often more relaxed and curious.

Sometimes, sharks will be circling the boat before the crew have dropped anchor, while other times it may take several hours before they come to investigate. Once they do arrive, seeing great whites face-to-face underwater is rather like meeting a procession of A-list movie stars. Having seen them in films, on television, in newspapers and on the covers of magazines for years, suddenly there they are in the flesh, their enormous triangular dorsal fins slicing through the water more professionally than those of any movie shark. Watching them is utterly addictive.

Life aquatic: Marine iguanas are the only seafaring lizards

Following in
DARWIN'S FOOTSTEPS

Ecuador: Galápagos Islands

Within minutes – if not seconds – of landing almost anywhere in the Galápagos, you are face-to-face with some of the tamest wildlife on the planet

The experience

What? Astonishing encounters with fearless, curious and mostly endemic animals

Where? Charles Darwin's 'Enchanted Isles' in the middle of the Pacific, 620 miles west of mainland Ecuador

How? Cruise from island to island in a small boat, then snorkel or explore on foot

Probably the most famous wildlife-watching destination in the world, and the place that provided the inspiration for Charles Darwin's earth-shattering theory of natural selection, the Galápagos Islands need little introduction. A land of stark lava formations, cactus forests, lush green highlands, turquoise bays and quintessential tropical beaches, this extraordinary archipelago flaunts wildlife at every turn.

Roughly 620 miles off the coast of Ecuador, and slap-bang on the equator, it consists of a cluster of volcanic islands sitting on a hotspot in the earth's crust where three constantly shifting tectonic plates meet. It is only five million years old and – judging by recent volcanic activity – it's still under construction. Cruising past in a boat, the term 'moonscape' often seems more appropriate than 'landscape'.

There are 13 islands larger than four square miles, plus six smaller islands and over 100 islets. Every island has its own unique atmosphere, distinctive landscape and inimitable wildlife. Not only are many species endemic to Galápagos, they are often endemic to a specific island – so the more islands you visit, the more variety you are going to see. One day you could be watching timeworn giant tortoises in the misty highlands, and the next you could be snorkelling with playful sea lions in crystal-clear water. You could be sunbathing on black lava rocks next to prehistoric-looking marine iguanas, or sitting with waved albatrosses as they perform their bill-circling, swaggering courtship displays (rather like Samurai warriors performing *Lord of the Dance*).

It's almost impossible to exaggerate the wonder of the Galápagos. Strewn across every conceivable space – in the shallows, on the beaches, along the footpaths – is more awesomely tame wildlife than

anywhere else in the world. You can see everything from penguins living in the tropics and boobies with bright-blue feet to tool-using woodpecker finches and male frigatebirds turning their wrinkled throat sacs into inflated red balloons.

In many ways, it's much the same as when Darwin first set foot in the archipelago, back in 1835. But there are changes afoot. Insatiable demand in Asia for sea cucumbers and shark fins has spawned widespread illegal fishing activities that are devastating the once-rich surrounding seas. A rapid rise in immigration, combined with exponential economic growth, has brought lots of people to the islands (the resident population has swelled to more than 30,000, living on four different islands). And they have brought with them excess baggage in the form of alien mammals, insects, plants and diseases that are threatening the archipelago's fragile ecology.

Perhaps the most conspicuous change in recent years has been in tourism. The number of tourists has quadrupled from 40,000 a year in 1991 to more than 160,000 today. In certain places, at certain times, the well-worn paths can be as busy as high street pavements. But it's not all doom and gloom. There are still quiet corners of the archipelago and the wildlife is just as approachable as it was in Darwin's day.

Most visitors have a top-ten wish-list: Galápagos penguin, flightless cormorant, blue-footed booby, waved albatross, magnificent frigatebird, Darwin's finch (any one of 13 species), Galápagos giant tortoise, marine iguana, Galápagos sea lion and Galápagos fur seal. Everything else is a bonus. They are all endemic except for the blue-footed booby and magnificent frigatebird, which are pretty much everywhere and become a familiar sight early on in the trip.

Penguins are found mainly around the westernmost islands, where particularly

Crustacean colour:
Sally Lightfoot crabs
scuttle about
everywhere around the
many Galápagos islands

Inset: The swallow-
tailed gull is the only
gull to feed at night

SPECIES CHECKLIST

- Galápagos sea lion
- Galápagos fur seal
- Humpback whale
- Bryde's whale
- Sperm whale
- Short-finned pilot whale
- Bottlenose dolphin
- Common dolphin
- Striped dolphin
- Galápagos penguin
- Blue-footed booby
- Red-footed booby
- Masked booby
- Common noddy
- Waved albatross
- Red-billed tropicbird
- Magnificent frigatebird
- Great frigatebird
- Lava gull
- Swallow-tailed gull
- Audubon's shearwater
- Lava heron
- American flamingo
- Galápagos rail
- Galápagos hawk
- Short-eared owl
- Galápagos mockingbird
- Floreana mockingbird
- Española mockingbird
- San Cristóbal
  mockingbird
- Darwin's finch
  (13 species)
- Galápagos giant tortoise
- Marine iguana
- Galápagos land iguana
- Santa Fé land iguana
- Española lava lizard
- San Cristóbal lava lizard
- Floreana lava lizard
- Galápagos lava lizard
- Green sea turtle
- White-tipped reef shark
- Galápagos shark
- Spotted eagle ray
- Sally Lightfoot crab
- ...and many more

"Galápagos giant tortoises grow to a ripe old age – some of the individuals alive now were probably around in Darwin's day"

cool currents keep water temperatures low. They can be seen in several different places, but only breed on Isabela and Fernandina. These two islands are the only breeding grounds for flightless cormorants, too; as their name suggests, they can't fly, but they use their vestigial wings to balance when jumping from rock to rock. Waved albatrosses breed only on Española and nowhere else in the world (apart from a few pairs on Isla de la Plata, near the Ecuadorian mainland); they are present between April and December.

Darwin's finches are probably the most famous birds in the archipelago. As a result of his five-week stay, Darwin speculated that the 13 species of these rather unassuming little birds had evolved from a single species on the mainland – and this set the stage for his major breakthrough. Each species has evolved to exploit a particular niche, with highly specialised feeding strategies and beaks.

But perhaps the best-known of all the inhabitants is the Galápagos giant tortoise. Growing up to five feet long, and with its wizened head, telescopic neck and toothless grin, it looks like a creature from a different era. There were once believed to be as many as 15 different sub-species, with considerable variations in size, shell shape and habitat preference, but four have become extinct since people arrived (the total population has declined from over 250,000 to about 15,000 today). They grow to a ripe old age and most probably

get to celebrate their 100th birthday; some of the individuals alive now were probably around in Darwin's day. The best places to see Galápagos giant tortoises are in the highlands of Santa Cruz and on Alcedo Volcano, Isabela, which host by far the largest populations; there are other, smaller populations on San Cristóbal, Santiago, Española and Pinzón.

The final must-see species is the marine iguana, the only sea-faring lizard in the world. There may be as many as 300,000 marine iguanas across the Galápagos Islands and they are impossible to miss. Loafing around in the sun to raise their body temperature between dives, they strike a familiar frozen pose atop lava rocks, and frequently 'sneeze' brine out of salt-excreting glands in their nostrils.

The seas around Galápagos are teeming with life and snorkelling here is terrific. This is the best way to encounter sea lions, of course, and there are many good spots for them. Fur seals are a little harder to find, but there are one or two places (the seal grotto on Santiago is the best place to view them up close). There are also opportunities to snorkel with penguins, flightless cormorants, marine iguanas, green turtles and more than 300 species of fish. You are likely to see anything from spotted eagle rays and yellowtail damselfish to sharks: white-tipped reef are the most familiar but, if you're lucky, you may come across black-tipped reef, Galápagos, hammerhead and even whale sharks.

But it's not just where you go – it's *when* you go. Wildlife activities vary greatly month to month. For instance, green turtles begin egg-laying in January; penguins interact with swimmers on Bartolomé from May to late September; humpback whales begin to arrive in June; July to the end of September is the best period for most seabird activity; peak pupping for sea lions is around August, while pups play aqua-aerobics with snorkellers in November; December is when giant tortoise eggs hatch. There is always something going on.

There are more than 60 approved visitor sites across the archipelago. Here are a few of my favourites:

Right: The Galápagos has lots of everything – sea lions flop on the beaches, giant tortoises lurk in the highlands, masked boobies keep a close eye on proceedings

Below: The Galápagos hawk surveys its island home

I've had so many 'best days' in the Galápagos Islands, it's hard to know where to begin. But I think my overriding memory is of snorkelling with sea lions and penguins in the shadow of Pinnacle Rock, on Bartolomé. The penguins kept surprising me by 'flying' past at great speed, before disappearing out to sea. But the highlight was one particular sea lion that performed relentlessly, turning somersaults, blowing bubbles and streaking by so close it almost (but not quite) touched me. There were turtles, too. They would have been the highlight of a snorkel in most parts of the world – but they didn't really get a look in.

Santa Cruz (Indefatigable)

A huge dormant volcano, in the heart of the archipelago, Santa Cruz is where most Galápagos tours begin. It's not far from the main airport, on Baltra, and its capital, Puerto Ayora, is the most populated settlement.

The prestigious Charles Darwin Research Station is a short walk from Puerto Ayora and is the place to learn about the island's natural history and the conservation work of the Charles Darwin Foundation. It also has a giant tortoise breeding programme, where baby giant tortoises are reared. Best of all, it is the retirement home for Lonesome George,

the archipelago's most famous resident and the last survivor of the Pinta Island giant tortoise sub-species. Look out for Galápagos rails, no fewer than nine species of Darwin's finches, Galápagos mockingbirds, vermillion flycatchers and many other birds.

A trip across the highlands of Santa Cruz takes you through agricultural fields and up into the bird-rich misty forests. If you listen carefully, you can hear wild giant tortoises crashing through the undergrowth – and, with a little luck, you will see one. Don't forget to look out for woodpecker finches: one of only a few tool-using birds, they use cactus spines to lever out grubs.

Santa Cruz also has some excellent snorkelling: the best places are Punta Estrada and Bachas Beach, but Tortuga Bay and Las Grietas are also good.

Santa Fé (Barrington)

Halfway between Santa Cruz and San Cristóbal, Santa Fé is much flatter than most other islands in the archipelago. With a glorious turquoise lagoon, and fine sandy beaches, it is the quintessential tropical island.

There are several Galápagos sea lion rookeries here and this is one of the best places to snorkel with these playful animals in calm water. There is also a nice trail, meandering through a forest of 30-foot-tall prickly pear cacti, where you might see the endemic Santa Fé land iguana. This is a good place for Galápagos hawks, too, which are very approachable when they are perched on the cacti. Views from the top of the cliffs are sensational.

Floreana (Santa Maria or Charles)

One of the oldest settlements in Galápagos, Floreana was attracting pirates and whalers long before the influx of tourists.

At Punta Cormorant, on the north coast, there are two beautiful beaches (one has sand so fine that it could be mistaken for flour) where green turtles nest, from January to May. There are American flamingos in a secluded brackish lagoon in between.

Devil's Crown, an eroded volcanic cone nearby, is fabulous for snorkelling. There is a good chance of close encounters with Galápagos sea lions, green turtles, octopuses and curtains of colourful fish. You may even see a hammerhead shark, if you are lucky.

It's also worth a stop at Post Office Bay, for the big wooden barrel that doubles as a do-it-yourself postal service. Established by British whalers in 1793, it is still in use – visitors continue the long tradition of

Above: The archipelago has several species of inquisitive mockingbirds

Below: The best place to snorkel with Galápagos penguins is off the beaches of Bartolomé

dropping off letters here for others to pick up and post when they get home.

Española (Hood)

This is the most south-easterly island in the archipelago and is best known for being the only place where waved albatrosses breed. There are about 12,000 pairs nesting on the cliffs at Punta Suárez, from April to December, alongside masked boobies. Española also harbours the largest nesting colony of blue-footed boobies in the archipelago, as well as lots of marine iguanas and lava lizards along the shore. A blowhole that shoots water some 65 feet into the air adds a dramatic touch to the scene.

Gardner Bay, in the north-east, has a powdery white sandy beach that is home to a colony of Galápagos sea lions – and this is a great place to snorkel with them. It's also a primary nesting site for green turtles and there are lots of colourful fish further out towards Tortuga Rock. Inquisitive Española mockingbirds will check you out on the beach, while Española lava lizards scuttle around your feet.

San Cristóbal (Chatham)

San Cristóbal is home to the provincial capital, Puerto Baquerizo Moreno, and has several good wildlife sites.

It is possible to see both magnificent and great frigatebirds at appropriately named Frigatebird Hill, with a beautiful view of the bay below. El Junco Lagoon, in the highlands, is the only freshwater lake in the Galápagos, and is good for waders and

wildfowl. Punta Pitt, on the north-east coast, is one of the few places where it is possible to see all three species of Galápagos booby nesting.

You get the usual sea-lion welcome here, plus San Cristóbal mockingbirds, Darwin's finches, vermillion flycatchers, San Cristóbal lava lizards and marine iguanas.

Santiago (James or San Salvador)

Santiago comprises two overlapping volcanoes and is the best place to see endemic Galápagos fur seals (which occur at few other visitor sites). James Bay, on the west coast, is the place to head for – the fur seal rookery is just beyond the rock pools at Puerto Egas.

Puerto Egas has a long lava shoreline with various wonderfully eroded rock formations. Marine iguanas bask in the sun and land iguanas feed on exposed algae. It also offers some of the best rock-pooling in Galápagos, with Sally Lightfoot crabs, hermit crabs, sponges, the endemic four-eyed blenny and lots of shorebirds (many unusual migrants have been recorded here). Look out for woodpecker finches, various Darwin's finches, vermillion flycatchers, Galápagos hawks and doves, and a variety of other birds. If you're really lucky you might see a Santiago Galápagos mouse, which was believed to be extinct until its rediscovery in 1997. It's also a good place for endemic Galápagos snakes, which are about three feet long and non-venomous.

There is some very good snorkelling here, too, with sea lions and – if you're fortunate – fur seals.

Bartolomé

Bartolomé is home to one of the most recognisable landmarks in the Galápagos: an eroded, volcanic tuff cone called

Looking for love:
The magnificent frigatebird
inflates his neck pouch to
attract the ladies

"Hike Bartolomé's Walk, a sandy trail through an otherworldly landscape, all the way to the 375-foot summit: the views are breathtaking"

Above: The 13 finch species helped inspire Darwin's theory of evolution

Below: Though the flightless cormorant has lost the ability to fly, it still dries off its wings after every dive

Pinnacle Rock. The white, sandy beach below is great for snorkelling, with penguins, green turtles, sea lions and myriad tropical fish.

There is lots of other wildlife in the area: blue-footed boobies, red-billed tropicbirds, lava herons, vermillion flycatchers, marine iguanas and Sally Lightfoot crabs among them. If you walk to the back of the beach and across to the bay on the other side, you may see lots of juvenile white-tipped reef sharks, which often mill around in the shallows.

It's also worth hiking Bartolomé's Walk: up a series of wooden steps, along a sandy trail through an otherworldly lava landscape, all the way to the 375-foot summit of the island (known as Heartbreaker). Do it before breakfast, in the cool of the early morning and in the best light, when the views across two beautiful bays are breathtaking.

Isabela (Albemarle)

The largest island in Galápagos, Isabela is made up of six large volcanoes, five of which are active. Wolf Volcano, which lies bang on the equator in the north-eastern corner of the island, is the highest point in the archipelago at 5,600 feet.

This is *the* place for Galápagos giant tortoises. There are far more of them on Isabela than on any other island – nearly 10,000 altogether. There is a different sub-species on each of five volcanoes: Sierra Negra (500), Cerro Azul (700), Darwin (1,000), Wolf (2,000) and Alcedo (5,000). The misty highlands of Alcedo, reached by quite a considerable hike, are probably the best place to see them. They spend much of their time wallowing in shallow, muddy pools in the caldera.

Isabela is also one of only two places (the other being Fernandina) where Galápagos penguins and flightless cormorants nest. Elizabeth Bay, on the west coast, has more Galápagos penguins than anywhere else in the world.

Urbina Bay, further north, has marine iguanas and some of the largest and most colourful land iguanas in the archipelago. It is also a good place to see penguins and flightless cormorants. Tagus Cove, further north still and facing Fernandina, is also worth visiting. There is a beautiful walk up to Darwin Lake, for superb view over its green saltwater lagoon and across to Darwin and Wolf volcanoes. It's a good place for bird watching, with finches, mockingbirds and Galápagos hawks much in evidence.

The nutrient-rich waters off the west side of Isabela are as good as anywhere in the entire archipelago for whales and dolphins. Humpback whales and bottlenose dolphins are most commonly seen, but a variety of other species turn up from time to time.

Finally, snorkelling at Punta Vicente Roca can be very good for marine iguanas – possibly the best place to see them grazing on algae underwater.

Fernandina (Narborough)

In the far west of the archipelago, Fernandina is one of the less-visited islands. It is nonetheless spectacular – rising to a height of about 4,600 feet, with a caldera some four miles across. And it is one of the best places for some of the most iconic wildlife.

It is one of only two islands (the other being Isabela) where Galápagos penguins and flightless cormorants nest. The rocky area around Punta Espinoza, in the north-east, is the best place. You can also follow a trail into some lava fields (so full of fissures they are surprisingly tricky to walk over) to a large colony containing literally hundreds of marine iguanas. It is reputed to be the densest colony of marine iguanas anywhere.

Want to play? Sea lions welcome visitors to almost every island, lolling on beaches and frolicking in the waters

Need to know

WHEN TO GO

There is **no wrong time to visit** – each month has its own highlights. The hot, humid, slightly **rainy season** (occasional tropical showers) is December-May (March and April are usually hottest and wettest); the seas tend to be calmer and clearer (60-80 feet visibility), so this period is best for snorkelling (water temperature averages 26ºC [79ºF]). The cool, **drier, windier season** (occasional drizzle or mist) is June-November; sea temperatures drop to as low as 19ºC (67ºF) and visibility to 30-50 feet; sea swells can make some landings tricky. The busiest periods are December-January and July-August. Check individual wildlife seasons, as they are all different (and vary during El Niño).

HOW TO DO IT

Fly from **Quito or Guayaquil**, on the Ecuadorian mainland, to **Baltra** or **San Cristóbal**. Some cruises leave from Baltra (the dock is a five-minute drive from the air terminal). Others go from Puerto Ayora, the tourist hub on Santa Cruz (a 10-minute ferry ride followed by a 45-minute bus journey); this is a bustling town, with a bank, ATM, taxis, pubs, a cinema and a choice of hotels.

The only practical way to explore the Galápagos is by **live-aboard boat**, travelling between islands mostly at night and making different stops each day (there are countless combinations). A **two-week trip** will allow you to explore most of the key visitor sites (including the outer islands). Most cruises go ashore twice a day: 10 days on the boat typically means 20 shore landings, 10-20 snorkels and several panga boat rides on about 10 different islands. Go ashore as early as possible, to avoid other groups and to see the peak of animal activity in the best light. Visitors must be accompanied by a **licensed naturalist guide** at all landing sites.

Alternatively, you can stay on some islands. Santa Cruz, San Cristóbal, Floreana and Isabela have **hotels** of various sizes. A few boat operators offer day-trips.

Tower (Genovesa)

One of the more distant northern islands, Tower is as flat as a pancake. Darwin Bay is the top spot here: created when the island's large crater collapsed below sea level, it provides a dramatic backdrop for thousands of seabirds.

You go ashore on a sandy beach and follow a trail along salt bush and mangroves, where there are nesting blue-footed and red-footed boobies, magnificent frigatebirds and red-billed tropicbirds. Keep your eyes peeled for Galápagos doves, as well as sharp-beaked, large cactus and large ground finches, and even short-eared owls (an endemic

sub-species). The beach has the ubiquitous sea lions, and sometimes fur seals. The snorkelling occasionally turns up hammerhead sharks.

Prince Philip's Steps, on the eastern side of Darwin Bay, is a good place for panga (small motorboat) rides, with a plethora of seabirds. The trail takes you past nesting masked boobies and blue-footed boobies on the rocks, with frigatebirds and vast numbers of red-footed boobies in the trees. A lava field lies at the end of the trail, where clouds of wedge-rumped storm petrels fly around en masse (even in daylight – unlike storm petrels elsewhere). This is another good spot for short-eared owls.

ACKNOWLEDGEMENTS

I would like to say a special thank you to **Lyn Hughes**, Editor-in-Chief of *Wanderlust* magazine and a great friend for many years, who loved the idea for this book from the outset and has been a huge and enthusiastic support throughout. Thanks also to the brilliant **Dan Linstead**, editor of *Wanderlust*, for nurturing and guiding the project through from start to finish. Lyn and Dan also did a wonderful job with their editorial expertise in cleaning up the manuscript. Huge thanks to the rest of the Wanderlust team, as well – **Graham Berridge** (Art Director), **Danny Callaghan** (Operations Director), **Sarah Baxter** (Associate Editor) and **Tom Hawker** (Production Editor) – for doing such an outstanding job and being such a pleasure to work with. Due to pressure of work and travel and things, I missed the deadline (or maybe it was a result of spending so much time with Douglas Adams, who famously loved the 'whooshing sound' deadlines make as they fly by?) and yet they were always patient and enthusiastic.

I would also like to thank some intensely knowledgeable friends and colleagues who are fortunate enough to live and/or work in my favourite places around the world. They very generously gave up their valuable time to comment on the chapters (though any errors that remain are mine alone, of course). They are (in alphabetical order): **Doug Allan, Giuliano Bernardon, Asbjorn Bjorgvinsson, Jennifer Covert, Cathy Dean, Caroline Fox, Nick Garbutt, Chris Genovali, Paul Goldstein, Greg Grivetto, Pete Oxford, Paul Paquet, Ian Redmond, Fiona Reece, Sandra Seth, Bibhab Kumar Talukdar, Michael A. Uehara, Leigh Ann Vradenburg, Frank Willems, Sheri Williamson** and all the wonderful staff at **New Zealand's Department of Conservation.**

Thank you very much to my great friend and co-conspirator, **Stephen Fry,** for writing such a generous foreword and for being such an enthusiastic and entertaining travel companion on trips to the world's greatest wildlife places.

Writing a book is a mostly solitary and often lonely process, but it is made palatable by the support and encouragement of friends who, from time to time, manage to drag me out of the house and into a café, restaurant or rugby match to talk about anything but wildlife and travel. I am thinking particularly of **Roz Kidman Cox, Peter Bassett, John Ruthven, Nick Middleton, Harry Hook** and my lifelong friend and confidante, **Debra Taylor.**

Special thanks go to **Rachel Ashton,** my astute and ever-thoughtful manager and unwavering friend. Rachel toils away behind the scenes, making everything possible.

And, last but by no means least, a huge thank you to my wonderful parents, **David and Betty.** They have done more than words can say.